Praise for *See It. Say*

Dr. Hellerstein's considerable experience in using visualization to enhance the visual process as an optometric practitioner is the basis of this book. She provides her model of visualization and the means to implement it to foster success in school, athletics and other real life situations. Her target audience is parents and teachers. However, the contents of this book is of significant value to other professionals who seek to improve the quality of life of their patients. These include optometrists, psychologists, physical and occupational therapists.

—Irwin B. Suchoff, O.D., D.O.S., FAAO, FCOVD
A Distinguished Service Professor, Emeritus
State University of New York, State College of Optometry

Dr. Hellerstein has provided invaluable information regarding the benefits of visualization whether you are in the field of education, an aspiring athlete, or a concerned parent. As a college professor working in teacher education, I look forward to using this book with pre-service teachers in order to equip them with the background knowledge and important practical application of using visualization techniques in helping every child move toward academic success. As a parent, I will use these strategies with my boys as they face rigorous academic and athletic challenges daily."

—Vicki Nilles, Ph.D. Candidate
Assistant professor of teacher education at Metropolitan State College,
Educational Consultant, Parent

If your child struggles with self-esteem and confidence, you'll love See It. Say It. Do It! *Dr. Lynn Hellerstein has created a practical and down to earth guide for helping your children tap their inner emotional and intellectual resources. When kids feel good about themselves they naturally perform better. This book will take you step-by-step through the process of helping your children transform negative thoughts, images and feelings into positive affirming ones that result in successful behavior and feelings of greater confidence. Dr. Hellerstein shows you how to incorporate these strategies naturally into everyday activities.* See It. Say It. Do It!—*an easy-to-read book overflowing with powerful life tools!*

—Deborah Sandella Ph.D., R.N.
Psychotherapist, *Releasing the Inner Magician*

Having worked with amateur and professional athletes alike, this book is a must read for all individuals involved in meaningful movement. The information, techniques and activities in this book benefit our children on every level of life's learning journey.

—Sue Lowe, O.D., FCOVD
Past Chair of the American Optometric Association Sports Vision Section

As a family, we feel Dr. Hellerstein saved my daughter and gave her a future of endless possibilities. When Alexi hit a wall in third grade (academically her work plummeted, emotionally she was falling apart and her self-confidence was non-existent) I was told I had too high of expectations and she was "average at best." I knew in my gut this was far from the truth and I pursued help from outside resources. Thankfully, I was referred to your office. After 4 months of vision therapy and visualization strategies, she thrived academically (well above her peers), read like a fiend and her self-confidence blossomed. Today is she is in middle school, thriving in the gifted program in both language arts and math. We could not have done it without you. We are thrilled with our experiences. They have truly been life changing for our girls. Thank you, thank you, thank you!

—Jennifer Wenger, Parent

Hooray! Dr. Lynn Hellerstein has created an exciting, fun and positive model for assuring students' success from the inside out. Since the first time I went on an amazing hot air balloon ride with her in my mind's eye over 20 years ago, I have been impressed with her understanding of visualization. Capitalizing upon over two decades of clinical experience, Dr. Hellerstein really understands how teachers and parents can help their kids develop the important visualization skills necessary to read with comprehension, write coherently, play sports proficiently, and behave with confidence. Her See It, Say It, Do It! *Model should be an inherent part of education from pre-school through the high school years, in public, private, parochial and home-school settings.*

—Patricia S. Lemer, M.Ed., NCC
Executive Director, Developmental Delay Resources (DDR)
EnVISIONing a Bright Future

American author, Alfred A. Montapert, noted that, "to accomplish great things, we must first dream, then visualize, then plan.believe.act!" Or as Dr. Lynn Hellerstein states in her new exciting book on visualization, See It. Say It. Do It! *She covers the topic of how to use visualization to improve the student's response to the world as it challenges, stresses, and pushes them to act. Teachers, clinicians, parents and all who interact with children will find this book useful in helping a child achieve their goals. Visualize this book being in your hands today. Now act on that visualization. You'll be glad you did!*

—Dominick M. Maino, O.D., M.Ed., FAAO, FCOVD-A
Professor of Pediatrics/Binocular Vision, Illinois College of Optometry

This is a book that all teachers and parents would benefit from reading. Teachers need to know that often poor readers aren't generating visual images in their minds from the text. When this skill doesn't come naturally—it has to be taught! Standard reading programs don't always address visualization techniques. Children need to see pictures in their head in order to re-tell a story or write a story. This book will be a most valuable addition to educational material.

—Shirley Osorno, M.Ed.
Retired teacher and school administrator

If you're a parent, share this book with your friends. If you're a professional, use it as a blueprint to expand your views about vision. I began the book wondering if it was ahead of its time, and finished it with the realization that its transformative power is timeless.

—Leonard J. Press, O.D., FCOVD, FAAO
Optometric Director, The Vision & Learning Center, NJ

Dr. Hellerstein is a world-class optometrist and vision therapist with pioneering expertise. She has written See It. Say It. Do It!, *whose format is easy to read, access, and understand. As a Physician's Assistant with 30 years of experience, I hear concerns from many parents about their children's school performance. I strongly recommend this book to parents, educators and therapists whose children are challenged by learning at school and who want a guide to using visualization for success and confidence in everyday situations.*

—Daniel T. Kamlet, PA
Partners in Pediatrics, Denver, CO

This method has "kid magic." Dr. Hellerstein delineates the child's mystifying process of creating visual images, transferring the elements to paper, and putting out his unique words to the awaiting world. This child has then left his mark. The pride and the satisfaction reveal the essence of the child's spirit while the finished product shows a flash of his soul. The sequential steps of the See It. Say It. Do It! *establish a memory for success. Every educator and parent must reference this book for the success of our youngsters.*

—Patricia Atwell
Tutor/Academic Coach/Educator

Through the years, as a parent, teacher and vision therapist, I have witnessed how visualization greatly impacts children's learning, as well as impacting my own personal confidence. If more parents and teachers utilize the tools in Dr. Hellerstein's book, See It. Say It. Do It!, *they will find visualization as useful as I do.*

—Stacie Ryman M.A., COVT
Retired teacher

Reading problems are frequently tied to vision problems; the eyes must be able to focus correctly at reading distance. Dr. Hellerstein has treated children with vision problems for years and teaching them wonderful visualization techniques. She shares these important learning tools with us in this wonderful book! Parents and teachers will be thrilled with her insight into learning. I know I will be referring to her book often in my tutoring practice!

—Claudia Earley: M.A. in Spec. Ed.
Private Reading Tutor

This is a valuable resource in bridging the school-home gap. It reinforces for educators the importance of visualization to all students and gives parents step by step examples of how to encourage and implement visualization practice.

—Laura Hamilton
Meadow View Elementary, Enrichment Teacher

I believe it to be a very useful resource for parents and teachers and hope to use techniques you have taught us in teaching this year. Thanks for your enthusiasm, guidance and care and support through the years. You have taught me personally new ways to look at my world and care for my family. You are a blessing Lynn.

—Krystal Kaes
Parent of child in vision therapy, Home Educator

In her book, Dr. Hellerstein provides an insightful overview of the role visualization plays in learning. Her practical activities make it easy for teachers and parents to implement theory into practice providing children with a powerful learning technique. For those of us who continually search for ways to help struggling children reach their potential, this book will be a useful guide.

—Betsy Kutrumbos, Ph.D., Educational Counseling Services

Dr. Hellerstein has cracked the code to learning for all types of students; visual, auditory as well as kinesthetic type learners can gain insight and inspiration from the stories and examples given by Dr. Hellerstein. See It. Say It. Do It! is an easy read, no nonsense approach to learning, communicating and just plain being successful in all areas of one's life...in and out of the classroom, sports field, and boardroom! Parents, teachers, coaches and people who just want to improve their daily communication and effectiveness should make this book a must read!*

—Audrey Boxwell, Ph.D.

SEE IT.

SAY IT.

DO IT!

The Parent's & Teacher's

Action Guide to Creating

Successful Students

&

Confident Kids

DR. LYNN F. HELLERSTEIN

www.HiClearPublishing.com
Centennial, Colorado

Books may be purchased for sales promotion and for volume pricing by contacting the publisher:
HiClear Publishing, LLC 7180 E Orchard Rd, #103, Centennial CO 80111
303-850-9499 • 303-850-7032 Fax • Info@HiClearPublishing.com

Cover Design and Illustrations by Annie Harmon
Interior Design by WESType Publishing Services, Inc., Ronnie Moore
Illustrations by Shannon Parish with the exception of those on pages 193 and 198
  by Jared Torgerson

LCCN 2009935488
ISBN 978-0-9841779-0-5

1. Education.   2. Vision Therapy.   3. Parenting.
4. Developmental Vision.   5. Behavioral Optometry.
6. Success in Children.

First Edition   Printed in Canada

To Motts & Potts

You lived your vision of *family*.
Your gifts of love, courage, and acceptance
inspired us to transform into confident individuals.
Thank you for creating a loving family.
"Stick Together!"

Contents

Dear Parent and Teacher ...   xiii

Foreword   xvii

Introduction   1

Part One
Visualization ... The New Frontier   **9**

  1. What is Visualization?   11

  2. Your Child's Vision Development   23

Part Two
See It. Say It. Do It!—**The Model**   **39**

  3. See It!   41

  4. Say It!   57

  5. Do It!   69

  6. Ta-Dah!   89

Part Three
School Readiness & Skills   **97**

  7. Why Kids Aren't Ready   99

  8. Learning to Sequence   105

  9. Developing Visual Information Processing Skills   117

10. Reading Opens a Whole New World   131

11. Acing Spelling   141

12. Creative Writing Can Lead to Anywhere   151

13. Math Can Be Fun   163

14. School Stressors—Homework and Tests   171

15. Improving Performance in Sports and Music   185

Part Four
Personal Growth   **203**

16. Building Self-Confidence   205

Dr. H's Final Insight ...   215

Appendix: About Vision Therapy and Patient Survey   217

Endnotes   225

Vision Resource Center   229

Glossary of Vision Terms   233

Acknowledgments   237

About the Author   239

List of Activities

Chapter 1

Take a Hot Air Balloon Trip   18

My Ape Is ...   20

Chapter 3

The Light Bulb   41

Scrunch and Relax   47

The Dog Shake   48

Belly Breathing   50

Building Awareness   55

Chapter 4

A Declaration—Exclaim It   61

Lazy 8 Thumb Rotations   66

Cross Marches   66

Chapter 5

My Car Is Stuck   74

Practice Goofing Up!   76

Chapter 8

The Creep	106
Following Directions	112
Going on a Picnic	113
Bunny Hunt	114

Chapter 9

Peanut Butter and Jelly Sandwich	119
Parquetry Blocks	121

Chapter 11

Spelling—See It, Then Write It	144

Chapter 12

Write About Your Pictures	153
Creative Writing Exercise: Mind Mapping	158

Chapter 13

Math-Fact Strategy	167

Chapter 14

Get Rid of the Clutter	172
The Clock Is Ticking!	177

Chapter 15

Sports Preparation Visualization for Young Kids	191
Sports Preparation Visualization for Older Kids	192
Sports Preparation Visualization for a Team	197

Chapter 16

The Confidence Movie	210

Dear Parent and Teacher ...

As I have watched my patients grow, develop and succeed as adults and now bring *their* children in for vision care, the satisfaction of making a difference in a person's and a family's life has been immensely gratifying. After my 30 years as a developmental optometrist in private practice, I grew tired of hearing the stories of frustration, anger, and poor self-esteem that so many children struggle with—and unnecessarily so. It is my desire to share my years of experience and lessons from my patients, therapists and teachers that has motivated me to write this book.

When I think of the power of visualization and the great successes I've had with thousands of patients using these strategies, I am truly excited to get *See It. Say It. Do It!* into your hands. Imagine your children having powerful tools to help them learn and increase their personal growth and development. Imagine that they are given the opportunities to learn these tools early in life, so that they can develop, build, deepen and enhance their abilities for lifetime learning while loving life and building solid relationships. Watch them grow and blossom. You will be giving them a gift for life!

This book is for every parent whose child struggles in school, or gets stressed before taking a test, or lacks confidence dealing with situations and classmates. It's for parents who envision more for their children and want them to get the best possible start in life. It's also a resource for teachers to augment and invigorate their current lesson plans.

See It. Say It. Do It! outlines a model for success. It is more than just a primer on "visualization." It gives you a step-by-step process to help your child achieve the school goals—and life goals—that your son or daughter needs. Along the way, you both will gain knowledge and resources about the critical link between vision and learning. I developed the *See It. Say It. Do It! Model* and have been using it in my vision therapy practice for many years. I have seen the results and they are astounding.

This book also exemplifies how the power of the *See It. Say It. Do It! Model* can transform you personally. It did for me. I was a workaholic who thought I was quite proficient at balancing the stresses of a successful practice and those of raising a family. However, my life took a dramatic turn when I encountered a medical crisis in 2002 that threatened my physical and emotional stability.

I found it difficult to think clearly, work, or be productive. I felt that I had crashed and burned. All the work, the accolades and awards, and my successful business partnership, which seemed to define who I was, were no longer priorities. Because of this health crisis, I lost my confidence and sense of who I really was. I searched for answers, physically, emotionally, and spiritually. My journey during this time took me through traditional and non-traditional medical and healing resources. I didn't realize it, but I was being given the opportunity to "reevaluate" myself and my life.

Through all of those treatment modalities, I was able to learn, heal, and rebuild my life. My experiences with visualization and the *See It. Say It. Do It! Model* through my vision therapy practice was a major component in *my* healing. I discovered how vast and powerful its potential is in expanding one's life, even in the midst of trauma, pain and instability.

I now am making choices on my life's journey from a totally different perspective, from a more balanced approach, balancing my passion with peace, through visualization and intuition. I have been given another chance in life and want to make the most of it.

My mission is to make a difference in this world, empowering individuals by teaching them to explore their internal and external vision.

Let's start with you and your child!

I am grateful for the opportunity to share my experiences, discoveries, and the magnificent results. I am honored by the praise and thanks I receive from my patients, and thrilled that their vision is improved, and now have renewed confidence and are enjoying life a lot more. Their futures look bright.

Now, when I hear, "Thanks so much, Dr. Hellerstein!" I know a good part of that thanks goes to the development of visualization skills. Thank you to all my patients. Without you I would not have visualized this book!

With love and compassion,
Lynn Fishman Hellerstein

Foreword

The opening lyrics of a very famous song by The Beatles, begins with the following invitation:

> Picture yourself in a boat on a river
> with tangerine trees and marmalade skies.
> Somebody calls you, you answer quite slowly
> a girl with kaleidoscope eyes.

How do we do that? By that I mean, how do we picture ourselves doing anything? *Lucy in the Sky with Diamonds* was John Lennon's creation based upon a drawing shown to him by his son, Julian, about a little girl in his class, Lucy. John knew intuitively that we each have the power to create mental images in our mind's eye. We call that *visualization*. Can that potential be harnessed for something other than the creative arts? This is the critical question that Dr. Lynn Hellerstein sets out to explore.

In the introduction to his marvelous book, *The New Executive Brain*, Elkhonon Goldberg poses a challenge. How does one write about topics of the brain that maintain balance between informing a scientific and professional audience, and being accessible and entertaining to a wider readership?

When my good colleague, Dr. Hellerstein, first told me of her ambitious project in writing a book about visualization, the same thought crossed my mind. How would she manage to write a book about a complex topic that would inform professionals, yet be useful to the general public? After having had the pleasure of reviewing her manuscript, the answer became clear. Dr. Hellerstein orients her book directly toward parents, and professionals will be well served in understanding how parents acquire tools that can shape their child's ability to visualize.

Lynn, as she would want you to call her, is at her best in sharing insights on how visualization has helped shape her career as well as raise her children. In her model, visualization is a bridge that helps create successful students and confident kids. As powerful as visualization can be, however, Lynn is clear that it is only the first step in achieving transformation, or change in the way one goes about accomplishing things. From your viewpoint as a parent, the steps in this process involve the child seeing the task ahead, articulating those points, and then doing something about it. A professional description would be: visualize, declare and take action. From the child's perspective it is simplest to remember: See It. Say It. Do It!

Our world is becoming increasingly more visual. Computer software applications have hastened the move toward icons, and pictures have literally become worth a thousand words. So the ability to "see it" or visualize it will become increasingly more valuable. Visualize, for a moment, the features of a stop sign. What color is the background of the sign? What color are the letters? Are they upper case or lower case letters? How many corners does the sign have? You know this information not because you memorized it, but because you can see the sign in your mind, as clearly as if it were in front of your eyes, and you can say or enumerate its properties.

Seeing it and saying it sets the stage for doing something with it, "it" being information or concepts being communicated. As Lynn notes early on in her discussion, the communication can be internal or external, and she makes a very nice distinction here. It is one thing to be able to turn pictures over in one's mind, but inability to communicate what appears in your mind's eye may earn your child the label of dreamers or ADD. Lynn provides valuable tips on how to help your child undergo this critical transformation from a wistful dreamer into a productive do-er.

One of my favorite parts among many in this book is the discussion about reading. I would venture to say that for most developmental optometrists working with children who are struggling to succeed, reading performance is high on the list of parental concerns. Visualization during reading is a two-way process. In creative writing, for example, the author begins with images, concepts and pictures in mind, and selects the language that best conveys this to the reader. The reader, in seeing the words, must reverse the process as the language triggers images, pictures, and concepts.

Young children begin reading with picture books, where the artistry tells a story supported by words. As children progress through the school years, the pictures diminish until chapter books take over, primarily consisting of words. Just as you are reading this and supplying your own pictures of what I just described, teachers expect your child increasingly to generate images in their mind in elementary and middle grades. For some children who are challenged to visualize, being asked to do this is like learning a foreign language. You'll learn through this book how to guide your child's imagery through various fun procedures and specific projects.

It is easy to spot adults who were likely good visualizers in school. They are the ones curled up with a book, who find little else more relaxing. When they see a movie based on a book they've read, they're likely to express disappointment in what has been left out, or the actor selected to portray the starring role. In contrast, poor visualizers rely on someone else having put the action together and can't imagine how others would take more pleasure in reading a book than in seeing a movie.

One of the greatest gifts you can give your child is the gift of self-confidence. But children need much more than hollow praise, or simply being told they're good at something that they know they're not. You will therefore find yourself coming back to this book again and again to apply its principles. Envisioning how to handle different situations, ranging from test taking, to reading other people's intentions, to planning simple trips or life's choices; these are bonding experiences that will pay dividends as your child learns how to use this valuable tool we call visualization.

If you're a parent, share this book with your friends. If you're a professional, use it as a blueprint to expand your views about vision. I began the book wondering if it was ahead of its time, and finished it with the realization that its transformative power is timeless.

Leonard J. Press, O.D., FCOVD, FAAO
Optometric Director, The Vision & Learning Center
Fair Lawn, New Jersey

Introduction

Does your child struggle in school?

Is your child less than enthusiastic about learning?

Have you noticed how stressed your child becomes when it is time for test-taking?

Does your child lack self-esteem and confidence? Is he bullied?

Do you feel that your child may not be reaching her highest potential?

Would you like to empower your child to develop his or her own easy and fun strategies for learning?

Welcome to the world of visualization. This book describes what it is, how you use it, and what it can do for you if you learn to use it well. Visualization is easy to learn; we all have the rudiments of it and already are visualizing to some degree ... even the youngest of children.

Children are naturally curious, and they want to learn and explore. As toddlers, they are enthusiastic and love learning. Just watch a two-year old getting into everything in the cupboard, pulling things apart, laughing, questioning. He's having a good time.

But what happens when this youngster begins the formalized process of school? Why do so many eventually dislike and even resent school? What might you do as a parent—or teacher—to help bring the spark back into learning while also helping to reinforce skills in problem solving, reasoning and personal growth?

Let's take reading as an example. Reading is one of the most critical skills necessary for lifelong learning and success. Most young children love to be read to. They look forward to the bedtime ritual of their parents reading them their favorite stories each night. Copies of *Goodnight Moon* and *Curious George* are worn out because children fall in love with the characters and the theme. "Read it again, Mommy," "Read it again, Daddy," is echoed from household to household.

Today, though, too many children struggle in the process of learning to read on their own although they still love to be read to. *What is happening here?*

Good readers report they often "see movies in their heads" when reading; that is, they visualize the story as it unfolds. Sometimes they see themselves in the story. Children who don't like to read rarely experience seeing movies, imagining the story or seeing themselves within it. When a child says that reading is "boring," trust him, it is—letters and print are boring to him. Nothing has sparked his imagination ... yet.

When you read to your child, it is far easier for him to picture the story, just like a movie. There is no struggle to figure out words or letters. The characters come to life. Think about all the little boys that morphed into Luke Skywalker as he fought the evil Darth Vadar in *Star Wars*. Or in *Harry Potter*, when boys imagined being Harry, and girls, Hermione, with their magical powers. Remember how the tiger-striped cat grew into Professor McGonagall?

One of the greatest challenges is when a director takes a writer's work and converts it into a movie. He has to visualize what the author meant. When Hagrid takes Harry Potter on his first visit to Diagon Alley, they go through a dark, ancient door in the streets of London. Harry and Hagrid step back into times past, into what is a pub. Exiting the pub, Hagrid enters an enclosed brick way. With his umbrella, he taps on a brick on the wall in front of him. It magically pulls apart and Harry and Hagrid step into a whole new world:

bats, owls, goblins, magic wands and wondrous broomsticks. Harry is in awe. And so is the viewer. The director has created a movie that has become a children's classic, out of J.K. Rowling's *Harry Potter and the Sorcerer's Stone*. This is visualization at its best.

However, if your child has struggled in learning to read, and then undertakes the reading experience, he spends most of his time figuring out what the words are. He doesn't even get a chance to fall into the story; much less visualize what's going on or what could happen. In the *Harry Potter* scene above, a struggling reader would miss the nuances that the director of the movie was able to take from the book and deliver on the screen with such pizzazz.

If reading becomes a challenge and non-enjoyable, your child will most likely resist reading, and avoid any homework requiring it. Frustration grows. As a parent, you can observe his frustration; but often it is masked by avoidance behaviors.

You will learn several strategies in this book that introduce and use visualization techniques. I'll share activities to develop and enhance your child's learning skills and life skills in the areas of—

- *Academics*: reading, creative writing, spelling, math, homework, and test-preparation;

- *Sports*; and

- *Personal development*: stress management, handling fears, dealing with bullies, and building self-confidence.

Who Can Visualize for Success?

Everyone! You are visualizing, even though you may not be aware of it. Picture yourself on your dream vacation. Are you lying on a white sandy beach, cruising through the Greek Isles, or sitting in Fenway Park watching the Red Sox beat the Yankees? Guess what? You are using your visualization skills!

The ability to generate and use imagery begins when children are very young. Think about toddlers and pre-schoolers. They invent names, animals,

situations and almost anything to keep their active minds going. This all comes
from developmental experiences. Visualization skills are developed in the
young child just as are coordination and other cognitive skills.

A note about the term *visualization*: Some people think of
"new age" when they hear the word *visualization*. It is now
a topic found in science books and is beginning to be
taught in mainstream schools and sports. Anyone can use
visualization principles; it does not require a belief in any specific religious
or spiritual entity. Rather, a commitment to enrich your experience and
knowledge, along with keeping an open mind, are the necessary
ingredients to explore visualization strategies.

Some people visualize quickly; some do it easily; some don't know if they
visualize; some visualize with tremendous detail; and some have an awareness
or feeling but don't see visual pictures.

Empires have been built based on a person's ability to visualize—they see the
big picture. One of the biggest was created in 1955. Six thousand people were
invited to the Grand Opening of Disneyland—twenty-eight thousand showed up
because the buzz was that Disneyland was the place to be. And it was!

Walt Disney was a visualizer; he saw every detail of Main Street, Frontier
Land and the Magic Kingdom. He called his process "imagineering." Imagine
what it took to create Disneyland and later, Disney World and Epcot Center!
Walt Disney died in 1966. His visions continue to live long after Disney World
was birthed. When someone said to Mike Vance, the creative director of Disney
Studios, "What a shame that Walt didn't live long enough to see all this," with
an amused look, Vance replied, "But he did see it. That's why it's here."

What Disney did was take a visualization step, and that's what you're doing,
by building your child's awareness, as well as your own, of his visualizations
skills. He, and you, will be amazed at what happens.

Think of it as building blocks. You first need a foundation to support any structure that is built. The *See It. Say It. Do It! Model* is the beginning of building your child's solid foundation. The visualization activities are the tools to help him get there—to become a successful, confident student. As your child practices visualization more frequently, and trusts the process, he begins to "see" success and have a lot of fun, whether it is at school, in sports, or in social situations. The *See It. Say It. Do It! Model* revealed, becomes a habit and part of his everyday routine. I knew I was on target when one of my 10-year-old patients wrote,

> I can enjoy life now because I can get through anything
> without having to stop and wait to understand it. Answers
> come much more easily, as well as imagery in books. This has
> opened up my eyes (no pun intended) to a whole new world.

When your child starts to use these tools and strategies and incorporates them into his everyday life activities, the benefits will stay with him forever—you've given him a gift for a lifetime.

How to Use This Book

This book is made up of four parts. Each section includes Activities to support its specific theme. The first part explores what visualization is and how it develops. In the second part, the *See It. Say It. Do It! Model* is introduced. The model was developed in my optometric practice. The acronym VDAT is the adult terminology for the *See It. Say It. Do It! Model*. It stands for Visualize, Declare, Take Action, and Transform.

Visualize is **See It.**

Declare is **Say It.**

Take Action is **Do It!**

The model leads to Transformation, which for your child is a huge **Ta-Dah!**

The third section includes specific visual processing skills and visualization strategies relating to school subjects that can help your child. Implementing them results in greater learning and confidence.

The final section provides a variety of topics that focus on personal growth, from getting along to dealing with scary and emotional situations.

A more thorough explanation of vision therapy as well as the results of our patient survey to evaluate effectiveness of their vision therapy is included in the Appendix. A glossary of vision terms and resources is also given.

Some of the chapters will have a numerical reference at the end of a sentence or paragraph. You will find details of a study or citing per the chapter in the Endnotes section at the back of the book.

I make suggestions on where these Activities can best be used throughout the book. Sometimes a road trip is a perfect place for one Activity; another might be at the dinner table, or just before a final bedtime goodnight. You'll also find **Dr. H's Insight** with each chapter—my "ahas" to you.

There are many books for adults on visualization, on business development, career goals, wealth development, meditative and spiritual growth. They are wonderful resources and I encourage you to use them for yourself if, after reading this book, you agree with me that visualization tools and practices can help on many levels and at any age.

I am surprised, however, that there aren't more books for parents and teachers about visualization for children. Since kids are on such a rapid learning curve, introducing visualization skills early in life gives them an advantage in schooling and social skills.

Special Note to Parents and Teachers

These activities are for use both at home and school. Teachers may want to include some of them in their school program or curriculum.

> If your child is struggling in school, consider having him tested for learning difficulties. In addition, make sure you have him evaluated by a developmental optometrist. Why would I suggest that? One out of four children has vision problems that could impact learning! I've seen miracles happen when children receive vision therapy for problems including: tracking, focusing, eye teaming, visual information processing, eye-hand coordination, even clumsiness and attention problems. It is amazing how reading fluency, handwriting, spelling, coordination and confidence improves when vision skills are addressed.

WARNING: *See It. Say It. Do It! Model* is not a substitute for vision therapy nor does it take the place of appropriate education.

Boys and girls can benefit equally from visualization skills and the strategies in this book. For simplicity, I use the words "he" and "she" interchangeably throughout.

If you have questions after you complete *See It. Say It. Do It!* or would like to relate experiences with visualization, please contact me. My information is at the back of the book.

Now, are you ready to learn and have fun at the same time? Then let's get going. The first chapter awaits you.

Part One

Visualization ...
The New Frontier

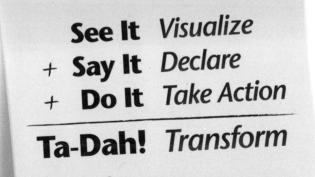

The *See It. Say It. Do It!*
Definition of Visualization:

The word, *visualization,* conjures up many images and meanings for people. Visualization is defined in numerous ways, depending on the person and the type of discussion and situation.

For example, *visualization* may be simply defined as utilizing visual mental imagery or picturing in your "mind's eye." Or the term *visualization* may refer to a more multi-sensory inclusive term utilizing seeing, hearing, touch, smell and taste imagery as well as body sensations.

The ability to imagine, sense, become aware of, move,
manipulate and expand the pictures in
your "mind's eye" and the feelings or senses in your body,
thereby developing new perspectives and creativity.

Visualization is the "knowing," or "I got it," or "gut feeling," through the orchestration of your senses.

1

What is Visualization?

Imagine this ...

Your plane descends after a long trip circling an island—your destination. You land and after some instructions from the flight attendants, you deplane and are greeted by a beautiful young woman who gives you a colorful, aromatic lei. You can feel the breeze and smell the salt in the air and the warmth of the tropical sun. Where are you?

It's Opening Day. The sun is out, the field is groomed, you hear the National Anthem being played, the crowd is packed, the vendors are selling hot dogs, peanuts and beer, and you can hear the organ playing "Take Me Out to the _____ ." Where are you?

The engines are roaring, you can see heat waves rising from the track and smell the fumes from the cars. The green flag signals the crowd that the race has begun. Where are you?

You are surrounded by excited children peering through fences. A woman is telling several families about the bird aviary. You see the monkeys swinging from limb to limb. You hear the roars of the hungry lions. Where are you?

If you responded Hawaii (or a tropical island), ballgame, Indianapolis 500 (or any auto raceway), and the zoo, you have experienced visualization.

Visualization techniques are used all the time in children's games (although they don't realize it). They also are used in business, sports, healthcare and schools; in other words, just about everywhere. Consider these:

- A popular movie in 2004 was *What the Bleep!* In it, Dr. Joe Dispera, the author of *Evolve Your Brain*, reports that the same parts of the brain light up on an MRI when a person looks at an actual object, or if he imagines the same object in his mind. The brain does not distinguish the difference between real and imagined experience.[1]

- Visualization affects your outcomes. Jack Canfield, in *The Success Principles*, writes, "Your ability to visualize your dreams will serve as a catalyst in their creation."[2]

- In *Golf Digest*, October 2000, it was revealed that Tiger Woods first started working with Dr. Jay Brunza, a psychologist, who coached him on techniques for relaxation, visualization and focusing. He taught him how to enter into his "Zone," where he was able to achieve peak performance. Tiger Woods' experience echoes baseball great Yogi Berra, who said, "90 percent of this game is half mental."

- Researchers at the Mayo Clinic in Rochester, Minnesota, found that guided imagery can help you use the full range of your body's healing capacity. They are exploring utilizing guided imagery for the treatment of cancer, preparation for surgery, chronic stress and headaches.[3]

- Harvard University researchers found that students who visualized in advance, performed tasks with nearly 100 percent accuracy, whereas students who didn't visualize achieved only 55 percent accuracy.[4]

If you examine the success principles of Tiger Woods, Yogi Berra and Jack Canfield, you'll find that a common denominator is visualization. The lesson: create and use the image that leads to the action that will bring you what you want.

For kids, that result could be earning a good grade, making a new friend or scoring points in basketball. For you, it could be getting a promotion or going on a special vacation. For children and adults, it also includes gaining self-confidence, happiness, and a personal peacefulness.

Visualization Has Deep Roots

Is visualization something that twenty-first century scientists dreamed up? No! Visualization is as old as the hills. In fact, there are references to imagery as far back as 348 B.C. when Aristotle theorized that "man cannot think without mental images." But now that we are discovering it is a skill, we can actually train and develop ourselves to get the things we want or become the person we want to be.

And there is science behind it. Previously we thought that most of our learning occurred when we were young and it went downhill from there. Scientists and doctors continue in their research that shows that our brains change and are able to learn new things even as we age. The original belief was that only children had malleable brains—adults were stuck with what they had. In *Train Your Mind, Change Your Brain* by Sharon Begley, she cites multiple studies that show that the brain can change, including that of a mature adult. Neuroplasticity is the term used to describe this phenomenon. It means that the brain has the ability to change with learning.

One Learning Style Doesn't Fit All

Different types of learning styles have been identified, most simply described as visual-spatial, auditory-sequential, or tactile. Most children as well as adults have a preferred learning style, but in general, it is not at the exclusion of the other styles. The individual must be able to integrate and use his entire brain for learning and performance.

Observe your child's responses, body actions, and language. He often shows you what sensory system he relies on most frequently—indicative of his preferred learning style. For example, if your child starts his sentences with ... "Imagine that," "Picture this," "See you later," or "Did you notice?" he tends to process in a *show me* versus *tell me* manner. This child is a *visual-spatial learner*.

If he has more of an *auditory-sequential learning* style, you hear comments like, "I hear you," or "This doesn't sound right." If he reads well, he tends to assemble toys in a step-by-step fashion, per the instructions.

And if she likes to say, "Keep in touch," "This doesn't feel right," or "I have a gut feeling," she is a *tactile learner*.

Let's bring this home. What is your preferred learning style? If you bought a kit with all the parts for a new bookshelf for your family room, would you lay out all the parts and then proceed to read all the instructions beginning with #1, or are you someone who pulls out the screwdriver and hammer, rips all the bags open, dumps them on the floor and dives in—instructions, what instructions? And if you are married, what type of learner is your spouse? I confess, I'm the rip-the-bags-open, dump-everything-on-the-floor kind of person. Guess what type of learner I married? Interesting how opposites seem to attract.

Look at the illustration below. Creating the "bridges" between the different learning styles represented in the brain hemispheres (the two sides) is what we call bilateral integration. Many of the activities that you will learn about in the book are intended to build bilateral integration.

In the example of constructing the bookshelf, an integrated learner would start the task by utilizing her preferred learning style. In my case, I would just jump in and build the bookshelf by looking at the picture. However, if I ran into a problem, hopefully I would then refer back to the instructions, utilizing more of a sequential style to complete the task. The same thing should happen with a sequential learner. He may start with the instructions of attaching part A to part B. But if he runs into difficulty, he could look at the picture and gain information to help him figure out what to do next. This is the ideal scenario of integrated learning.

The reason that I bring this up is that you may be one type of learner and your child another. It's important that you understand this difference and be able to work with it. Otherwise, communications deteriorate and homework, for example, becomes a nightmare. In the classroom, if your child is more of a visual learner, and you find that his teacher teaches with a very auditory style, then your child may struggle in the classroom. The teacher may give an oral or written, step-by-step instruction, but your child doesn't get it. He needs to see it or be shown the activity.

Dr. H's INSIGHT

Visual-spatial learners see the whole picture. They tend to visualize patterns and connections—starting with larger concepts and seeing the final product. They are often creative, and don't learn well through a step-by-step process. They often skip over instructions and just want to "see" how to do it. These kids often struggle in a typical classroom that is structured in a sequential teaching style.

Auditory-sequential learners process more in a step-by-step, analytical methodology. They learn from part-to-whole with order, sequence and rules. The typical classroom is often taught in an auditory-sequential manner.

Tactile learners need movement and hands-on experience. Words are not as important. These kids are constantly touching and feeling everything.

Your child may be able to start a project. But does he have a strategy to use when he gets stuck? My experience reveals that many children just don't complete the task or get frustrated if they can't easily complete the task. This is most likely to occur because they don't look for or think of additional strategies to assist them.

This is not to say that one learning style is better or preferred over another, just different. All can visualize, but differently. Great companies need a mix of all types of learners, and most families have a mix as well. As a parent, you need to understand your child's learning style and help him to discover the tricks and tools to be successful.

I Don't *See* Pictures!

What am I doing wrong? I can't get it! All I see is black.

Don't create a situation of additional stress and frustration. If your child doesn't seem to notice the visual imagery, it doesn't mean he's not visualizing. It may be that he is aware through senses besides vision. As with different learning styles, visualization awareness differs. The language used to describe visualization and build skills also differs depending on the child's preferred learning style.

Your language of, "What do you see," or "Picture this," may give you no response. In that case, try changing your language when inquiring or leading visualization activities: "What do you feel" or "What are the sounds?"

Understanding the learning style of your child helps you adjust your language when asking him about his visualization. Use his *preferred language* when work-ing on visualization activities. The easiest way to eliminate problems is to ask multisensory questions using descriptors from all sensory systems.

A Blueprint

How can visualization help you achieve your goals? Call it a "blueprint." Instead of simply imagining or dreaming about something unrelated, imagine and allow a visualization to help you achieve your goals.

Now, apply this idea to your child. Let's say your child wants to earn better grades. He needs to do well on an upcoming spelling test. He pictures in his mind a sequence in which he studies using the visualization techniques illustrated in Chapter 11, *Acing Spelling*. He sees himself taking the test with confidence, seeing every word in his mind as he spells them. In his mind, he then pictures his teacher handing back his graded test with an "A" in her handwriting, at the top of it. He visualizes the steps necessary for him to excel, and sees himself excelling.

By repeating this visualization exercise often, what happens to him when he realizes that he can spell well and he is a good student and succeeds? A big **Ta-Dah!**

Up, Up and Away

For over 30 years, vision therapy has been my passion. It's no wonder that what I did within my office was mirrored at home. My daughters embraced the variety of visualization activities I use. One of my favorite Activities used with my children when they were young was to "take" an imaginary hot air balloon trip.

These trips helped my family create, practice, have fun, laugh and relax. It was the perfect antidote when they were worried about school or an upcoming athletic competition. They also provided a great opening for communicating with my children as issues with friends or school problems often would come up. We could "look" at the situation from our "balloon" and "see" possible resolutions for these situations. It was so successful when they were little, that the trips became a family staple, even as we are now all adults.

There are certainly many options to create your own personal balloon trip. Just keep emphasizing relaxing, breathing, quiet, safety and fun!

My balloon trip activity focuses on relaxation. You'll find more information on relaxation in Chapter 3, *See It!*

Try this one at home!

Activity
Take a Hot Air Balloon Trip

Purpose: Visualization for the whole family.

Try this as a bedtime relaxation activity or when preparing for a special event. The first few times you use this, you might read it to your child. Then have fun with it and create your own personalized version of a balloon trip.

Instructions to child:

Lie comfortably and close your eyes.

Imagine yourself blowing up a balloon—a big hot air balloon.

Notice the color of the balloon—what color is it?

(Pause)

Is it big or little?

(Pause)

Now take a big breath, allowing the air to fill up your belly (tummy), and then slowly allow the air to move out of your belly into the balloon.

Take another breath in, again feeling your belly rise, and then allow the air to move into the balloon.

Continue breathing in and out until your hot air balloon is just the right size for you.

(Pause)

Now, let's get into the basket connected to the balloon.

Is there anything you need such as a jacket, a hat, a seatbelt for safety, glasses for protection, your favorite blanket or stuffed animal?

(Pause)

Get comfortable.

When you are ready, allow the balloon to start floating up, going higher and higher and higher.

Continue to breathe deeply and relax.

Enjoy the ride as we go higher and higher.

Wave goodbye to your friends, your school and your homework. Put away any troubles or problems, as you continue to move higher and higher, up to the clouds.

(Pause)

Once you get to the clouds, you can get out of the balloon and play in them.

Touch the soft, fluffy clouds that support you and your balloon.

Smell the fresh clean air and cool breeze.

Feel the warmth of the sun, spreading throughout your entire body.

Listen and experience the quiet and calm.

(Pause)

See how far you can see, how the big blue sky goes on and on and on.

―――――∞――――――

As you continue to enjoy playing in the clouds, this balloon trip can go several different directions. For example:

You can practice any sport routine in the clouds, always knowing that the clouds will protect and keep you safe.

Or, you can snuggle up in the clouds and fall asleep.

You can get back into the hot air balloon and continue to another fun place, like candy land, or an amusement park, or any other place you would like to go.

Your child may want to come back home and land in his bedroom. Don't be surprised if you all doze off, and the balloon trip continues in your dreams.

Imagination Has No Boundaries

The following Activity taps the imagination—it's one that kids of all ages can do—it can be done almost anywhere. The sillier the responses, the better.

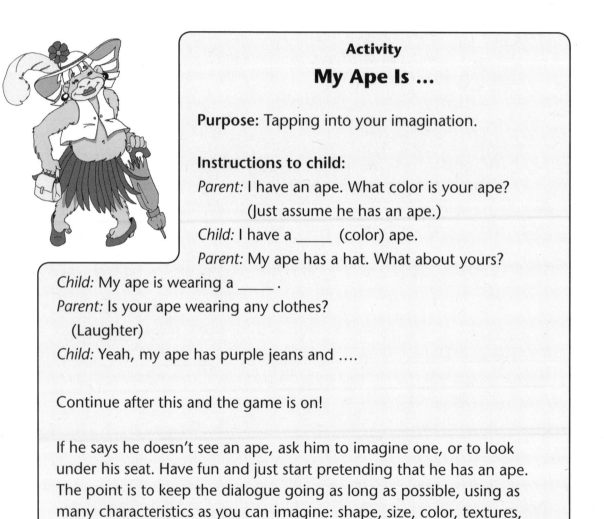

Activity

My Ape Is ...

Purpose: Tapping into your imagination.

Instructions to child:

Parent: I have an ape. What color is your ape?

(Just assume he has an ape.)

Child: I have a _____ (color) ape.

Parent: My ape has a hat. What about yours?

Child: My ape is wearing a _____ .

Parent: Is your ape wearing any clothes?

(Laughter)

Child: Yeah, my ape has purple jeans and ....

Continue after this and the game is on!

If he says he doesn't see an ape, ask him to imagine one, or to look under his seat. Have fun and just start pretending that he has an ape. The point is to keep the dialogue going as long as possible, using as many characteristics as you can imagine: shape, size, color, textures, clothing, objects ...

Garbage In, Garbage Out

There's a common expression used among computer enthusiasts which says, "Garbage In, Garbage Out." Well that's certainly at least as true for what we store and retrieve from our minds.

Let's tweak it, and make it a positive statement:

> *The better the quality of the information that our eyes take in, the better our mind's eye will be in using that information.*

In other words, since visualization relies on imagery through the mind's eye, we'll need to pay closer attention to how our eyes gather and process that information. This is where you discover how vision develops and integrates with other senses. Chapter 2, here we come!

2

Your Child's Vision Development

Everyone has senses. They are the "windows to our world." The big five are: seeing, hearing, smelling, tasting and touching. Of the five, vision is the dominant sense. It is estimated that more than 80 percent of all learning takes place through the visual system.

The techniques that professional athletes use to enhance their skills and performance are closely guarded secrets. I'm going to let you in on one of them. It's about tapping into their vision system and integrating what they see externally and internally with their other senses. This provides the blueprint for coordinating the movements necessary for the game.

Years ago, I had the opportunity of working with a Ladies Professional Golf Association (LPGA) golfer. Touted to be one of the best woman golfers of her time, she struggled her first few years on the Tour, failing to make the final cut for a golf tournament many times. Frustrated with her performance, which impacted her self-confidence, she began the journey to understand what was wrong. Eventually she was referred for a visual evaluation.

She was an excellent visualizer and would prepare for each putt by imagining her golf ball rolling over every blade of grass, flattening it and then imagining it springing back, as the ball traveled to the hole. Sounds good, but she had a significant difficulty coordinating her eyes. In other words, when she lined up for her putt, due to her visual coordination problem, she misjudged where the hole was.

What she was experiencing was a "Garbage In, Garbage Out" situation. When she saw it incorrectly (garbage in), she hit it incorrectly (garbage out). "My swing didn't feel the way it looked in my mind. There was a mismatch," she said.

When a sport involves eye-hand coordination, the motor movement is dependent on the accuracy of the visual information and the processing of that information. If my golfer misjudged the distance between the ball and cup, then her brain gave erroneous information to her motor system for the swing. The visualization she created prior to hitting her golf ball was inaccurate. Her body couldn't calculate the correct swing movement. Imagine the frustration that her putting created, not to mention all the tournaments and prize money she lost. She needed help.

Why 20/20 Vision Isn't Always Perfect

Contrary to the belief of many, vision and sight are not the same. Not only is there confusion within the general public, there is much confusion in the medical and education communities when it comes to sight and vision.

Here's the difference:

Sight merely refers to *eyesight* or *visual acuity.*
Vision refers to *seeing, processing and responding to visual information.*

Vision does not occur in the eyes, it occurs in the brain. The retina, which is the rear interior surface of the eyeball, is formed directly from brain tissue. It is here that the process of seeing begins. Many parts of the brain communicate with one another to create vision. There are different areas of the brain that respond, for example, to movement and to color. No one yet knows where or how all of the modules or pieces of vision come together into a unified picture. But we *are* sure of one thing: It doesn't happen in the eyes.

> Most children are born with healthy eyes, brain and nerves, but
> they have to learn how to use their eyes and coordinate them
> with the rest of their body.

The problem with finding and diagnosing children with vision problems is that many of them see 20/20. You as the parent, are told in vision screenings in school or at the pediatrician's office that your child has "perfect vision." All the child really has is 20/20 eyesight. She can see a certain size letter at a certain distance. Good, but not necessarily good enough.

I frequently examine children who have passed the vision screening, yet they have double vision or poor ability to track objects. When I discover a double vision problem in my vision testing, I ask, "Do you see double when you read?" The child responds, "Yes." The mother is shocked and asks, "Why didn't you tell me?" and the child responds, "Why didn't you ask me?" If that's how the child has always seen, she doesn't know enough to even complain about it. These kids often have significant vision problems, undetected by the vision screening.

How Do You Define Good Vision?

When it comes to explaining what it means for someone to have good vision, most people respond with one of the following:

- Ability to see 20/20.

- Having healthy eyes and not needing glasses.

- Ability to pass the school screening tests.

Although a child with good vision would have all of the three answers above, there is so much more to good vision. Your child needs to not only see clearly and have healthy eyes; he needs to be able to use his eyes comfortably, accurately and efficiently for long periods of time. In addition, he needs to be able to understand the information coming in and respond to that information.

Remember our LPGA golfer? Even though she could see 20/20, she couldn't accurately use her eyes together in a coordinated manner. This resulted in inaccurate hitting. She had a *vision* problem, even though she passed a typical vision screening. This illustrates the complex process of what we call *Vision*.

Think about what your child does on a daily basis. What are some of the signs of vision problems in kids? Most kids don't complain about a visual problem. They often just avoid activities or behaviorally act out.

The most obvious signs of vision problems you might see include: an eye crossing or drifting, squinting, covering an eye to see, funny head turn or tilt, rubbing his eyes, frequent blinking, or headaches after using his eyes.

Here are some possible consequences for a child with vision problems:

- Loses his place when he reads.

- Has difficulty remembering what she just read.

- Handwriting is sloppy with poor spacing.

- Struggles in sports; can't catch a ball, or is clumsy.

- Eye-hand coordination is poor.

Dr. H's INSIGHT

Your child may have 20/20 eyesight and still have a *vision* problem.

Use the following checklist to see if your child has vision problems.

✔ **Vision Checklist**

Carefully observe your child. Look for some of the more common signs of vision problems. If you check off several items, take your child for a thorough vision examination testing visual efficiency skills. Don't send your child to school without all the appropriate tools for learning success, especially visual skills!

Physical Observations:

____ One eye drifts or points "in" or "out," in a direction different than the other

____ Turns head to see

____ Head is frequently tilted to one side

____ Squinting, closing of one eye, or covering an eye

____ Excessive blinking

____ Poor eye-hand coordination

____ Frequently bumps into things

____ Fatigues easily

When Reading or Doing Homework:

____ Holds the book unusually close

____ Frequently loses place

____ Uses finger or marker when reading (after 2nd grade)

____ Rubs eyes during or after short periods of reading

____ Unable to read for long periods of time

____ Difficulty concentrating

____ Avoids homework

Behavioral Signs:

____ Headaches or eyestrain

____ Dizziness

____ Motion or car sickness

____ Visual complaints (blur, double vision ...)

The American Optometric Association recommends that your child have his first vision examination by an optometrist by age 1, then again by age 3, before starting kindergarten and then every year thereafter.

Basic Development

Is it possible vision problems may be the source of kids' learning difficulties? The answer is, YES! Yet many of these children pass the school screening. How do we detect these kids, so that they can receive the appropriate help?

Let's start by understanding the "Model of Vision" which emphasizes that vision is a learned process, and it is related to your child's development. How does that work?

Remember, most children are born with healthy eyes, brain, and nerves. Their visual skills are learned through a developmental sequence of movement and processing skills, starting in infancy (and before). Your infant and toddler's development has tremendous impact on his performance and abilities in school years later.

For decades, health care, child development and education specialists emphasized the integration of development of vision and movement. One of the great leaders in developmental optometry, Dr. A.M. Skeffington, said,

> Thinking is a movement pattern. Vision is a movement pattern.[1]

Dr. Homer Hendrickson, also a developmental optometrist, wrote,

> Movement has been called the key to learning, thinking and vision.[2]

Dr. Arnold Gesell, M.D., was a psychologist and developmental pediatrician. He authored several books including *The Child from Five to Ten*. His pioneering work created the Gesell Institute of Human Development in 1950. He created standards of predictable patterns of growth of development in young children. Today the Institute focuses on educating and supporting teachers and parents in a variety of areas including how children grow and learn. Dr. Gesell said,

> Vision is so fundamental to the growth of the mind that the
> baby takes hold of the physical world with his eyes long before
> he takes hold with his hands.[3]

When your child was an infant, she was totally dependent on you, for safety, feeding, and survival. She couldn't hold her head up. She couldn't do much besides eat, wet her diaper, cry, and fling her arms and legs. She had a few reflexive movements, which didn't require thinking, but were just a reaction. For example, if you touched her cheek, she turned her head toward you seeking a nipple to put in her mouth.

Her eyes didn't always focus well, and they might drift. Eye coordination came together between the fourth and sixth months. Eventually, her eyes looked straight and you didn't notice any crossing. This happens with the majority of children. However, some children end up with crossed eyes. Vision treatment may be required even with infants. This visual condition is called strabismus. To get more information on it, visit the College of Optometrists in Vision Development (COVD) website *www.COVD.org*, or the American Optometric Association (AOA) website *www.AOA.org*.

It didn't take long until she started gaining control of her head, sat up, rolled over and started smiling. She would look, following you around with her eyes if you moved. Her muscle development and coordination improved daily. From a visual perspective, this was the start of her learning how to fixate and track.

Her babbling intrigued you as you knew she understood what you said. It was as though she had something so important to say, but just didn't have the words to say it yet. This was the start of language development.

Then she started grabbing and touching anything and everything within reach. She didn't know that an object could be sharp or hot; she would touch it anyway. It was apparent that she was learning and exploring her environment. This was the beginning of understanding what she sees, and the development of her eye-hand coordination.

As she grew, she would put many of these objects in her mouth, feeling the texture, shape and form of these objects. I know this is always a scary time for parents because even the dirtiest and unsafe objects aren't excluded! This is part of the learning process. As she moved to a high chair, she would drop her spoon, over and over again, listening for the clunk as it hit the floor (and all the food that spills with it). She has now introduced depth perception to her world. How far and how long does the spoon take to travel? Where is it in space compared to me?

Then your daughter was ready to really explore her world. She needed to make purposeful movements to get from one place to another. She started scooting on her belly; eventually crawled; and before you knew it, she was walking when she was a 1-year-old.

And then, off to the races! Everyday brought new adventures, trials, and challenges. Your child grew, developed, and refined her skills as she approached the time to start for school. She learned to hold a crayon, a marker, a pencil; how to cut with scissors. All of these milestones happen with most kids if normal development takes place. But what if some of these milestones don't occur?

It Takes Time

As you can see, higher level thinking and processing abilities just don't happen overnight. Jean Piaget, a giant in the field of cognitive psychology in the mid 1960s, studied how the child's mind develops. Piaget believed in general stages of development. He believed that there were certain points at which development "takes off" and moves into completely new areas and capabilities. He saw these transitions as taking place at about 18 months, 7 years and 11 or 12 years. This had been taken to mean that, before these ages, children are not capable (no matter how bright) of understanding things in certain ways, and the idea has been used as the basis for creating school curriculum.

There are many, including Dr. Howard Gardner, a Harvard psychologist and author, who now questions the existence of general stages and structures. Rather, Dr. Gardner believes,

> That humans possess a number of relatively independent intelligences and these can function and interact in idiosyncratic ways.[4]

Development does not always progress in a smooth manner. All children develop at their own rate.

Dr. H's INSIGHT

Dr. Gardner still considers Piaget to be the giant of the field; his questions and observations are well respected.

Generally, the development of movement skills is learned from a gross to fine motor sequence. It comes with repetition and practice. Development of eye movement skills, like tracking a ball, or having accurate eye jumps along the page for reading, is dependent on a strong foundation of these gross and fine motor skills. Good eye movement skills are critical for building visual perception, higher thinking and processing skills. The integration of eye movement and body movement skills builds the foundation for learning and excelling at sports, as well as every day eye-hand coordination activities.

Look at all the important learning that has taken place even before your child walks into the classroom. If for any reason, your child had difficulties in any of the sensory or motor systems during her first years of life, this could set the stage for difficulties in learning. The child who has chronic ear infections may have difficulty learning phonics since the ears were often clogged when your child was first interpreting sounds. Or lazy eye might develop because your child had a significant difference in glasses prescription between her two eyes. Or, due to motor development delays, handwriting skills are difficult when it is time for school.

In my experience, these children often become frustrated, dislike school, avoid completing their work, and sometimes start showing behavioral signs, such as distracting others in class, not paying attention, cheating on tests, and not turning in homework. These kids often receive inappropriate labels in school such as, "slow learner," "attention deficit disorder," "learning disability," or "lazy."

Sending kids to school with vision problems is like going to work without the primary resources that you need for your job. Developmental visual skills are an essential part of school readiness.

The same thing can easily happen in sports. Watch the kid who is so excited to play but becomes frustrated very quickly. He can't seem to catch or hit the ball. Everyone tells him he sees 20/20. Then what's the matter? The coach jumps all over him for not paying attention, or swinging too soon, or just being a bad player. He feels stupid, not good enough, and might even want to quit the team (before he ends up spending most of his time on the bench). Or, he might develop inappropriate behaviors, like being the "class clown" to change the type of attention he receives. Little does he know that he has a vision problem that has not yet been diagnosed.

The Vision Model

Take a look at the illustration. This represents a Developmental Model of Vision. The outer circle represents the life activities that are important to your child: school, work, coordination/sports, play, relationships and success in life.

A strong *foundation* is required upon which to build. The *foundation* is represented as the central core of the concentric circles. This core includes the structural integrity of the vision system; that is, the physical health of the eyes, eyesight, and the visual pathways.

THE **DEVELOPMENTAL MODEL** OF **VISION**

LIFE ACTIVITIES
School • Sports • Work • Play • Relationships

VISUAL INFORMATION PROCESSING
Eye-Hand-Body Coordination • Visual Memory • Visualization
Spatial Perception

VISUAL EFFICIENCY
Follow (track) • Fuse (eye coordination) • Focus

PHYSICAL INTEGRITY
Fixate (look) • Visual Pathways • Eyesight
Eye Health

The first concentric circle outside of the core represents *visual efficiency*; i.e. how well the eyes fixate (look), follow (track), fuse (coordinate together), and focus (make objects clear). These visual skills are movement-based.

The second concentric circle out from the core represents *visual information processing* (understanding what we see, where things are in space, integration of visual information with other senses, eye-hand-body coordination, visual memory, and *visualization*).

This Model of Vision represents the basis for the evaluation and treatment for your child when he is examined by a developmental optometrist. As you can easily see, there is so much more than 20/20 eyesight to consider. Even if one eye doctor says your child has 20/20, it doesn't mean all these other vision skills have been appropriately evaluated. Read more about developmental optometry in the Appendix.

How do you find an optometrist who can provide a developmental vision examination? Ask you eye doctor these questions:

- Do you do "near point testing?"
- Do you give academically related vision testing?
- Do you provide vision therapy or refer to someone who does so?

If your eye doctor is not clear or doesn't do this type of evaluation, then you can find a referral for a developmental optometrist at the "Locate a Doctor" section of the website: *www.COVD.org*

When Kids Continue to Struggle

Early in my optometric career, I had great success in vision therapy based on a more structured model of vision, that is, treating basic eye sight and visual efficiency skills, but not including much work on *development, movement* or *visual information processing.* What changed my approach to vision care were the many children who were referred to me by excellent teachers, tutors, language therapists, and physicians as a "last resort." They referred kids who were still struggling in school, even though they received special academic assistance. These kids were frustrated and not performing well. They had difficulty just sitting in my exam chair long enough for me to do a vision evaluation.

I realized that all of my great, expensive instruments for vision therapy were useless because these children had such basic developmental and movement problems. To work with them, I expanded my model of vision, incorporating body movement and visual information processing into my vision therapy program. With this expanded vision perspective, I have now been able to treat many more types of patients, including:

- Those with basic developmental, learning and processing problems.

- Those who have poor vision efficiency skills: tracking, focusing and eye teaming.

- Gifted kids who have visual motor (eye-hand or writing difficulties) and often avoid completing their homework.

- Top athletes who want to enhance their performance.

- Children and adults who have visual problems after suffering a brain injury.

What happens if your developmental optometrist finds some difficulty in the above areas? There are a number of treatment options available, including glasses, contact lenses, vision therapy, ergonomic recommendations and other types of adaptations. Vision therapy is explained in more detail in the Appendix.

Here's an example of how appropriate vision treatment can impact a child.

Success Story

Everyone likes kudos. Imagine my pleasure when I opened the following letter which was sent to my office one day:

> Kevin completed eight months of vision therapy and is no longer experiencing eye fatigue and headaches. He reports to me that the letters no longer "jump around" on the page. Words are no longer blurry. He likes to read now, and, although still behind in his grade level, he is only a few months behind rather than 1½ years behind.
>
> I am a family practice physician and have realized how important developmental vision screening is for kids, not just simple vision screening. It is part of my routine now to really delve into school performance issues with my young patients to make sure they are progressing normally; otherwise they get referred to Dr. Hellerstein.

Since many children I evaluate have complex vision and learning issues, networking with other professionals has been a critical part of my practice; teachers, tutors, physicians, optometrists, speech/language therapists, occupational therapists, physical therapists, counselors, psychologists and others. I provide the best vision treatment possible, while utilizing referrals to other professionals when necessary. Maximizing your child's abilities is the goal!

It's no surprise that vision is our dominant system for learning. Look at the complexity of the visual system. Your child's eyes are truly essential in informing the brain about movement, and in using the mind for learning. And it's no surprise that kids struggle when there are unresolved vision issues.

Notice that the visual information processing part of the vision model includes *visualization*. If the foundation for vision and development are not solid, then your child's ability to *visualize* may be impacted.

Be preventative! Have your child visually evaluated.
If recommended, follow through on treatments your
developmental optometrist recommends.

The vision model is set. Now its time to learn how to use the *See It. Say It. Do It! Model.* Let's move on to Chapter 3, *See It!* and have some fun.

Part Two

See It. Say It. Do It!
The Model

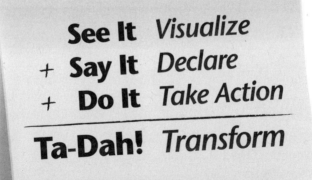

See It Visualize
+ Say It Declare
+ Do It Take Action
———————————
Ta-Dah! Transform

3

See It!

Visualization: The ability to imagine, sense, become aware of, move, manipulate and expand the pictures in your "mind's eye" and the feelings or senses in your body, thereby developing new perspectives and creativity.

Let's practice visualizing! It's not just about seeing a picture in your mind. The more sensations your child brings into her visualization, the stronger and more meaningful it becomes. Encourage her to turn her "lights on" with this next activity.

Activity
The Light Bulb

Purpose: Have fun using your many senses.

Instructions to parent:
When giving this visualization to your child, be sure to give her time to notice and describe her picture. Pause between questions. Don't feed her with answers. Let her have the time to imagine and create. It's not about having a right answer here. It's about your child learning to

continued on next page

---

become aware through all of her senses, and then to change, expand and create more pictures. Most kids love this activity and really get into the fun of it.

Some kids, however, have a different experience. You might tell her to see a light bulb, but she may see something else, like a tree, or a dog, or a color, or who knows what else. That is just fine. Go with it and explore whatever she sees. The goal is to start her becoming aware of her visualization process.

Instructions to your child

Parent: Sit comfortably, and take a few deep breaths.

(Pause)

Imagine a light bulb.

(Pause)

What color is your light bulb?

Child: It's ___ .

Parent: Now, change the color of the light bulb. Is it bright or dim?

Child: It's ___ .

Parent: Make it brighter, then darker.
   (With your hand, turn the light on and off with a flip of a switch or a turn of the dial. Encourage your child to actually "flip" the switch in her mind.)

Parent: Very carefully get close to the light bulb. Be careful, it might be hot!

(Pause)

Is the light bulb above you or on a table?

Child: It's ___ .

Parent: While looking at your light bulb, notice if there are any sounds in the room. Do you smell anything?

Child: I hear ___ .

Parent: Time to turn your light bulb out! "Click," there goes the switch.
   (Make a clicking sound representing a flip of the switch).

What if she reports that all she sees is black? No color, no light, no object, just black. That is fine too. Remember, there is no right or wrong here!

If she continues to report black or darkness, then ask her, "Make your picture blacker. In fact, don't let any light, not even a little, tiny light, move into your black picture."

Telling your child not to do something makes her do just the opposite, right? So if you tell her *not* to let light in, guess what happens? Kids will often report seeing colors, lights or something else. The key is to get movement and not stay stuck.

If the blackness persists, then have her move, jump, or bring in a body motion to "manipulate" and play in the darkness. See if it changes in any way, or not.

Remember, use no judgments about right or wrong answers. Just be there to lead her through her experience.

The language you use in these activities is very important. Ask about your child's observations; use language like, "What do you see? How do you feel? What do you notice?"

Do NOT ask your child, "Do you see it?" What do you think her response will be—NO! Just assume that she is making pictures. If she tells you she isn't, then ask her to pretend like she is.

Your Child Imagines All the Time

Some of the games that your child already plays can be used to practice visualization. Take jumping rope. Before your child goes in to jump, tell her to watch the turners turning. Tell her to pretend she is going in and feel her body jumping. Have her imagine bopping back and forth trying to time the turn, and the height of the arc. How high will she have to jump? Can she see and feel herself bouncing and clearing the rope? Until she can do this ahead of time, planning to be successful in this way, it's simply trial and error each time she jumps, along with several stumbles as she misses her "jump window."

Proceed then from this motor planning, through visualization, to taking action. And the "rule of the playground" is that once a child is successful keeping up a pace or rhythm, the turners will turn, "faster, faster." This, too, can be anticipated and visualized.

Proceed then from this type of "gross motor," to a fine motor board game such as checkers or chess, checkers being the simpler way to understand visualization. In checkers, all the pieces are equal until one of the players gets a King. Or, remember the scene in the first Harry Potter book when Harry, Ron, and Hermoine enter "The Chamber" and encounter a giant chess game? Neither Harry nor Hermoine have the skills that Ron does. He immediately visually assesses the situation, tells Harry and Hermoine to go to a certain spot on the chess board. He then mounts one of the knights and proceeds to instruct the chess pieces to move to other spots. Ron gulps, sweating as he declares the final movement that will enable Harry and friends to proceed.

The important point of these games is to visualize where to move; determine what the consequences of the move will be; determine the mental manipulation or rotation of the move that the other person will make and what you need to do next, until there is a conclusion to the activity.

If your child is not able to jump rope or play checkers, then choose a simpler activity, one that she can already perform. Make it a very easy task. Have her imagine herself walking up and down the stairs. The important lesson here is taking a few seconds to visualize before the activity starts.

Visualization Impacts

Practicing visualization opens another avenue. It prepares your child for an important aspect of socialization—empathy—being able to put himself in someone else's place. Children routinely "feel" the hurt when a friend is feeling low. And, if their friend loses a coveted toy, he can "see" and "feel" the loss.

As your child becomes a teen, the coveted prize they seek is a driver's license. Visualization drives driving. And, if a driver lacks it, they are a hazard to anyone and everyone in their path. Drivers have to anticipate what is to their right, to their left, behind them and what's coming. Much of success in driving safely hinges on how well you can visually assess, monitor, and anticipate. Any lack of visualization could lose a life.

As a parent, what can you do to integrate visualization into your everyday lives? Have fun with the activities; make them like games. Start with building his visualization skills in areas of his life that he already loves, like games and sports. As he builds confidence and success in his strategies, start bringing them into school-related subjects.

Remember, some kids see very clear, detailed images in their minds; like the Harry Potter descriptions used so far. Others don't see anything but they have a "body sense" or "gut feeling"; like completing a task and exclaiming, "that just feels right!" Some say they just have a sense or a "knowing," without any direct visual or body awareness. This is the "ah hah!" experience of just knowing and not being able to describe why or how it happened. When you help your child to become aware of his ability to visualize, you will notice him utilizing it in all areas of his life.

Enhance Your Visualizations: Relax, Breathe, Build Awareness

Relax

How do you feel when someone yells at you, **"RELAX!"** Are you relaxed? Or are you startled, tense, and holding your breath?

Relaxing is one of the key ingredients to great visualizing. Did you ever take a very important test; one that counts for your entire grade for your report card? You study, intensively, and then you get to the test; you are so stressed that you can hardly see the test, but you run out of time ... and you *really* do know all the answers. You know how difficult it is to concentrate on a task when you are harried or tense. Teaching your child how to relax carries a life-time benefit in all areas of her life.

How would you like your child to be nice and relaxed the next time she takes a test? So relaxed that she can read easily, think clearly and be resourceful? There's a great visualization in Chapter 14, *School Stressors-Homework and Tests* that addresses test anxiety. But let's start with relaxing. The secret is in the ability to do it.

Did You Know?	

When your body and mind are deeply relaxed, your brain-wave patterns actually become slower and more receptive to imagery. This means that a relaxed body and mind can potentially make far more effective changes in your life than all the thinking, worrying and planning that you do.

Let's get some practice in learning how to relax. The activity on the following page is designed to give your child a very simple physical experience.

Scrunch   **Relax**

Activity
Scrunch and Relax

Purpose: Learn how to relax.

Instructions to child:
Find a quiet, comfortable place to lie down or sit.
Gently allow your eyes to close.
Do you want a blanket to cover yourself, or a pillow to make you
  comfortable?
(Pause)
Start by tightening and relaxing your muscles.
(Show her how to squeeze her fists and then unclench them.)
Next, tighten your legs; now let them go.
(Pause)
Scrunch up your face tight, tighter, tighter! Now relax your face.
(Go through each body part, tightening then relaxing.)
Now make all parts of your body as tight as you can and count to five.
(Pause)
Relax your whole body by letting your muscles go soft.
(Pause)
How do your muscles feel when they are all tight?
(Pause)
What does it feel like when they relax?
(Pause)
Continue playing this game, refining which muscles to tighten and
  then relax.

Here's another fun activity to help your child learn how to relax. This is especially fun for young children.

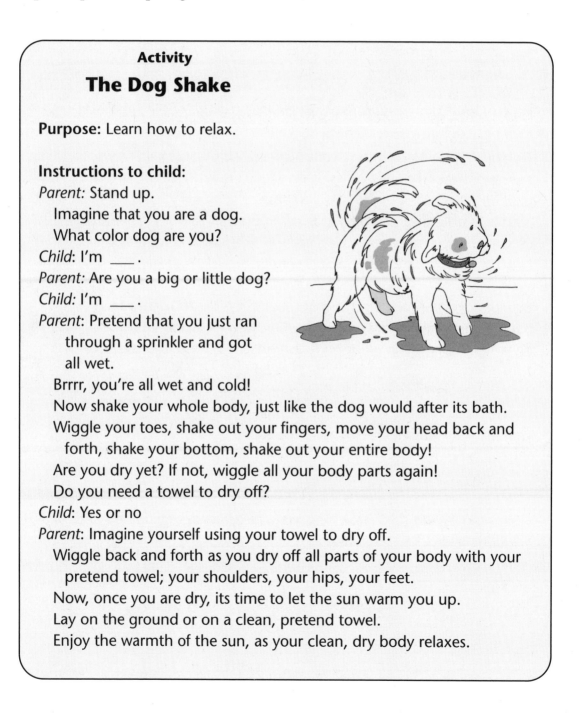

Activity

The Dog Shake

Purpose: Learn how to relax.

Instructions to child:
Parent: Stand up.
　Imagine that you are a dog.
　What color dog are you?
Child: I'm ___ .
Parent: Are you a big or little dog?
Child: I'm ___ .
Parent: Pretend that you just ran
　　through a sprinkler and got
　　all wet.
　Brrrr, you're all wet and cold!
　Now shake your whole body, just like the dog would after its bath.
　Wiggle your toes, shake out your fingers, move your head back and
　　forth, shake your bottom, shake out your entire body!
　Are you dry yet? If not, wiggle all your body parts again!
　Do you need a towel to dry off?
Child: Yes or no
Parent: Imagine yourself using your towel to dry off.
　Wiggle back and forth as you dry off all parts of your body with your
　　pretend towel; your shoulders, your hips, your feet.
　Now, once you are dry, its time to let the sun warm you up.
　Lay on the ground or on a clean, pretend towel.
　Enjoy the warmth of the sun, as your clean, dry body relaxes.

Breathe

Remember the last time your child had to have a shot? How about you? "This won't hurt," is what the nurse says—but you or your child knows better! What happens? Maybe you gasp; clench up; hold your breath? Almost anything but breathing and relaxing.

When you breathe deeply and teach your child how to do it, it creates calm, which is part of the relaxation process. And that aids visualization.

Most people don't pay attention to their own breathing. I notice that many of my patients hold their breath at times throughout my examination; whether it is due to fear of the procedure we're going to do, tension or anxiety. And I don't give shots!

Watch your child when he is angry or upset. Does he sometimes hold his breath, perhaps during a stressful situation? Does he sometimes breathe too fast? Or perhaps even hyperventilate or become winded?

Breath-holding interferes with our ability to function normally and automatically. Breath-holders often have chronic tension as well. This is of course not only true for children; it is true for adults as well.

There are two main ways you breathe; either from your belly or your chest. Belly breathing is the act of breathing deeply into your lungs by using your diaphragm, rather than breathing shallowly through your lungs and rib cage. This deep breathing is marked by expansion of the belly, rather than the chest when breathing. It is generally considered a healthier and fuller way to bring oxygen into your tissues.

Chest breathing is usually seen when someone is anxious, distressed or scared. You can tell when someone is breathing this way because the breaths are shallow and often irregular and rapid. The shoulders often rise up towards the ears. In contrast, belly breathing is like the more natural breathing of babies and sleeping adults. This pattern of breathing is more even and non-constricting. It is the easiest way to relax.

Belly breathing techniques on their own are very helpful in reducing anxiety disorders, panic attacks, irritability, muscle tension, headaches, and other stress related conditions. Below is a simple activity for both you and your child.

Activity

Belly Breathing

Purpose: Learn how to breathe from the belly (tummy).

Instructions to parent:
Find a quiet place where your child can lie down.

Instructions to child:
Shake out all your wiggles and just let all the tightness in your body
    fall away.
When you are ready, lie down, and make yourself comfortable.
(Pause)
Close your eyes.
Find your belly button and put one hand on it and the other hand on
    the center of your chest.
Simply notice how you are breathing. Which hand raises the most
    as you breathe in?
(Pause)
Slowly, make one or two full breaths out.
Just notice how you are breathing.
(Pause)
Now place both hands on your belly.
(Pause)
Continue to simply be aware of your breathing.
Notice your belly rise when you breathe in (inhale), and fall when you
    let air out (exhale).
Continue breathing through your nose, in and out.

If your child is having difficulty with this activity, try the following:

- Place a light weight such as a book on his belly so that he can see and feel it rise and fall.
- Place a support such as a pillow under his head.
- Have him bend his knees until they point up towards the ceiling and place the soles of his feet flat on the floor, hip-width apart.
- Have him turn over and lie on his stomach. It may be easier for him to notice his belly rising and falling because of the pressure from the floor on his belly.

Breathe In

Breathe Out

In Toluca Lake, California, children routinely participate in a class on breathing and relaxing. Sitting in a circle, they close their eyes, concentrate and breathe. After the teachers give them instructions, the children are told to notice how their bellies and chests rise and fall. Sometimes they would place stuffed animals on their stomach and watch the animals rise and fall. Belly breathing! Toluca is one the schools now using what is referred to as "mindfulness training."[1]

Belly breathing techniques are great for stress reduction. Explain to your child how he can use relaxing and breathing when he gets tense. Practice this with him regularly until he becomes comfortable with the strategy and it becomes automatic. Eventually he'll learn to belly breathe while he's sitting at his desk, standing in line or even waiting for a test. Then, when stressful situations occur, the belly breathing technique can be easily called on to reduce the nerves.

AHHHH! What a sigh of relief. Ever notice how you feel when you let out a sigh of relief? It's a great way to release tension. Try this: breathe in through your nose, and then just let your breath out your mouth. Do this again while saying "Ahhhhhhh." After you've tried it yourself, try it with your child.

Use belly-breathing strategies before undergoing medical procedures, during test anxiety situations or speaking presentations, when you are at the dentist getting a root canal, or in the doctor's office ready to get a shot. Put your hand on your belly and just breathe into your hand. Be aware of your hand going up and down on your belly. Just keep bringing your attention back to the breath and to your hand. This is a very effective strategy that can be used under the most critical situations. When your child learns belly breathing strategies, he takes a big step in learning to handle every stress.

Build Awareness

What happens when your child gets nervous? Does he get butterflies in his stomach? A headache? What does he notice happening to his body? Just have him notice all the little funny things that he feels in his body.

Becoming aware of ourselves—our body, our breath, our movements and feelings are essential to successful visualization. By paying attention to our body senses, we start to learn how to tap into our inner self vision and not be focused just on our external surroundings, our busy minds, or that television show. It's no different with your child.

When I was a kid, my sister called me a "turbo head." Some people define a turbo head as a workaholic. That was me. Not only was I constantly working on something, but I also had to deal with the judgments and chatter in my mind, like "Do it this way," "That will never work," "Are you good enough ... ?" It could be midnight, and my brain would still be on overload. My life was like an on-and-off switch. Either I was on—full speed ahead like the Energizer Bunny®—or I was out like a light, into a sound asleep. I sure accomplished a lot, but had a difficult time relaxing. There was never anything in between. Watching a movie was my time to fall asleep. Reading a book? That was a luxury for others. Could I have been your child?

When I hit my "wall" in 2002, my mind was far too busy to pay attention to what was really going on in my body. I knew I was on an unhealthy, stressful road, but didn't know what to do about it. Relaxing to "smell the roses" seemed like a waste of time.

I did recover from my personal medical crisis that year; my new healing process was about learning to listen to my body and trusting my intuition. I began to realize that my body had a great deal of information that I frequently ignored or resisted; like butterflies in my stomach, tingling in my heart, or tightness in my shoulders. When I started paying attention to my body sensations and its information, my confidence in my intuition grew and my decisions became easier and clearer to make. If I had a decision to make regarding taking on a project, I would see the possibilities, but I needed to also listen to my body as to whether it felt right as well. This new awareness greatly reduced the stress I had created for myself, as well as enhanced my joy and love for life. I discovered a new way of living my life. It all started with quieting my mind, relaxing, breathing and awareness.

What interferes with awareness? Fears. For me it was the drive to excel, to be the best and always be right, the fear of making a mistake. The fear of failure kept me from truly experiencing my life's journey; as I was just focused on the expected end result, and certainly not enjoying the process.

This happens to many children! We all have fears. How we deal with them is what allows us to either move forward or become stuck. Neither you, nor your child should have to take the journey I did to "wake up." Your journey should be in the present, starting with awareness.

Sam's Butterflies

Here's an example of how the awareness strategy helped Sam, a six-year old patient of mine. He came into the office upset and told my vision therapist that he was nervous about something that was happening at school. He didn't tell us what he was nervous about. It was hard getting him started on his vision therapy session, because of his current emotional state.

We asked him, these questions:

Vision Therapist: What does being nervous feel like? Just notice what is going on in your body.
Sam: I have butterflies in my tummy.
Vision Therapist: What color are they? How many of them are there? Are they big or little? Are they flying around? Do they make any noise? What happens when you watch these butterflies?

Did you notice that we didn't ask Sam what was wrong? Rather, we pursued his body awareness of sensations. Sam gave us some very detailed answers about the butterflies and the feelings in his body. Just bringing Sam's awareness to the actual physical sensation of the butterflies calmed him down. We then asked

Sam what he'd like to do with all those butterflies. He decided to let them float out of his body by imagining them like clouds just passing through.

Too often we want to "fix" the problem; we could have just pursued finding out what was wrong. That would have focused his concerns on *worry*, rather than on *relaxing*. Our message to Sam was that he didn't need to change anything. He needed to just be kind to his butterflies and himself. Once he calmed down, then he could share with his parents what he was so upset about.

Below is an activity that will build you and your child's awareness now.

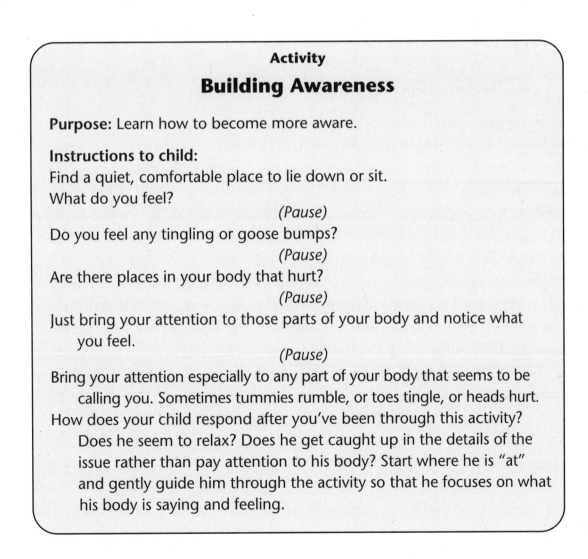

Activity
Building Awareness

Purpose: Learn how to become more aware.

Instructions to child:
Find a quiet, comfortable place to lie down or sit.
What do you feel?
(Pause)
Do you feel any tingling or goose bumps?
(Pause)
Are there places in your body that hurt?
(Pause)
Just bring your attention to those parts of your body and notice what you feel.
(Pause)
Bring your attention especially to any part of your body that seems to be calling you. Sometimes tummies rumble, or toes tingle, or heads hurt.
How does your child respond after you've been through this activity? Does he seem to relax? Does he get caught up in the details of the issue rather than pay attention to his body? Start where he is "at" and gently guide him through the activity so that he focuses on what his body is saying and feeling.

Summing Up

For both parents and teachers, the ingredients to be successful with visualization include:

- Understand your child's learning process

- Relax

- Breathe

- Build awareness

- Have fun

- Relate the activities to specific goals

- Be consistent in doing the activities

Remember, there is no right or wrong way to visualize. Your child's way is his best way!

Now that you know more about visualization, you may be tempted to jump right into the activities for specific academic subjects. Utilizing the entire *See It. Say It. Do It! Model* is essential. If you skip steps or just try pieces of the model, you may be successful, but your success may be limited. It would be like making your mother's favorite chocolate cake recipe without using all of her same ingredients; and then wondering why it didn't taste the same as mom used to make.

Let's now move on to the second step of the *See It. Say It. Do It! Model*, **Say It** loud and **Say It** clear!

4

Say It!

We hold these truths to be self-evident, that all men are created equal,
that they are endowed by their Creator with certain unalienable
Rights that among these are Life, Liberty and the pursuit of Happiness.
—From the Declaration of Independence

That's a declaration! The Declaration of Independence, a statement explaining the decision by Congress of the separation of the American colonies from Great Britain, was approved on July 4, 1776. This publically announced that the thirteen American colonies, then at war with England, were now independent states and thus no longer a part of the British Empire. The vision of independence came to fruition with the Declaration. What a powerful statement for all Americans to live by.

Declare it—**Say It** is the second component of the *See It. Say It. Do It!* *Model*. This means to say out loud what you want to happen; and say it like it already has come true. In other words, start with the end result and then work backward.

Declarations, also called affirmations, are important elements of the visualization process that lead to transformation **(Ta-Dah!)**. It is crucial to clearly and persuasively state the declaration of your vision. A strong declaration transforms your attitudes and expectations in life.

How does this relate to kids? Easy—kids say what they are going to do or not going to do. Read on about the power of their thoughts.

Your Child's Thoughts

Thoughts are one of the most powerful forces in your child's world. Thoughts are like sparks in the fire. They come and go quickly, unless they ignite and magnify. Who allows this to happen? Your child does. The more a thought is repeated, the more energy and power it generates. These thoughts influence every aspect of his life, his choices and attitudes. Your children (and you too) are a product of these thoughts.

As a parent, you want your child to have a good attitude, make wise choices, have confidence, and great self-esteem. Can you help him with this? Of course you can. Learn from the pros—golf superstar Tiger Woods, international bicyclist Lance Armstrong, basketball star Michael Jordan, tennis pro Serena Williams, and Olympic gold medalist Shawn Johnson. And that's just the tip of the iceberg in sports. Whatever industry you look at, the leaders use some form of visualization as part of their journey in their success.

How can you help your child manage his thoughts? Parents of my patients often share their concerns with me regarding their child's low self-esteem. A common statement, "I keep telling Johnny he's smart, but he doesn't believe me," is heard daily in my office.

The *See It. Say It. Do It! Model* is an active process to teach your child how to manage his thoughts. It starts with the visualization, and then the declaration toward a particular purpose. For very young children, you can read declarations to your child to empower him as well as teaching him the vocabulary. Kids love to hear positive statements about themselves. For example, if your child is nervous about taking a test for swimming, you could first say to him, "I am going to do well. I'm a swimmer." And then have him repeat that over and over again. As your child grows, he can then use these declarations with his visualizations.

Stating, "I am a winner" or "I am a great student" or "I'm going to do really well on my test" over and over again helps create that result in your child's mind, making it much more likely to happen. Keeping these thoughts in his mind, replaces the thoughts that he might have: "I'm stupid, I'll never be able to do this, Why bother ..." It is very important to replace the negative mind comments with strong powerful statements that are repeated over and over. Let the declaration be his, not yours; one that he sees and believes about himself, or at least believes is possible.

Have your child state the declaration in the present tense. Have him say, "I **am** a good student," not "I will be a good student" or" I might be a good student." Keep the declaration positive. Replace "I'm not going to avoid my homework anymore," with "I complete my homework every day." The simpler and shorter the declaration, the more effective and powerful it is.

If your child still procrastinates; gets stuck or even paralyzed because there's so much homework to do; or has the attitude, "I'll never finish it so why start"—the affirmation might not be "I'll complete all of my homework every day." This might be too big of a leap for your child to take. Rather, he might create the declaration, "I'll put in ten minutes on each of my homework assignments every night."

It's important to visualize something that seems very reasonable to attain. Then, if he exceeds it, he will feel great that he has accomplished even more than he set out to do, rather than feeling like a failure again. It's like motivating a person by dangling a carrot (or reward). The possibility of reaching the carrot needs to be reasonable, otherwise, if the carrot is dangled too far, it will look impossible to grasp—resulting in another failure.

Start with Small Goals

Start with small goals to build confidence and experience. Once your child experiences the confidence of visualizing, stating his declaration and having his goal happen, then encourage him to look at an even bigger picture, beyond just a test or simple activity. Go for the big dreams! Look at what big dreams can produce.

Imagine that you are back at the 1932 World Series. The Yankees are ahead of the Chicago Cubs by two games. Babe Ruth, the legendary New York Yankee, was up to bat. Hearing the rowdy crowd and jeers, the Babe stepped out of the batter's box and pointed towards the outfield bleachers, like stating a premonition of what was to come. On the following pitch, the Babe connected and sent the ball 435 feet, the longest home run ever hit at Wrigley Field. Babe Ruth had remarkably "called his shot!" Was it truly a called shot, or part of the Babe Ruth legend? No one knows for sure, but it makes you think about the power of a declaration. Babe Ruth certainly believed in it.

You may notice that I have used a lot of baseball analogies. This isn't by accident. I'm married to a man who so loves the game of baseball that in my household, according to the Gospel of Bruce, baseball is the metaphor of life. It follows the seasons—when things bloom, you have new promise, high hopes and eternal dreams.

In the classic film, *Field of Dreams*, Kevin Costner plays Ray Kinsella. He walks in his cornfield and hears a voice say, "If you build it, he will come." Looking around, he can't see where the voice comes from, doesn't know who "he" is, but sees a vision of a baseball field, right smack in the middle of his cornfield in Iowa! When he shares the voice and vision with his wife Annie, she is skeptical but supports him. To the disbelief of his farming neighbors, he declares that he will build the baseball field. He plows his corn under and builds his dream field.

A year passes before Shoeless Joe Jackson, a controversial player from the past Chicago "Black Sox" team, appears on the field. But only Kinsella can see him. Shoeless Joe represents the baseball bond between Kinsella and his deceased father. Kinsella discovers by the end of the movie that the field was built to restore his relationship with his father.

As you can guess, this movie is one of the Hellerstein classics. It's a terrific model for you to use with your kids, especially if they like sports. Ray Kinsella searched for his dreams; his dreams came to him in a vision. He discovered that even the impossible can come true. He saw it. He said what he would do. He did what he said. The field was built.

When your child says they can never be good at or never do this ... (fill in the blank), remember *Field of Dreams*. What separated Kinsella from many of his family and his friends was that he visualized a team playing in the field he built. Everyone else thought he was nuts. He believed in his vision and built it. Not only did the whole "Black Sox" team show up, eventually his own father appeared.

Let's develop declarations using techniques that created the *Field of Dreams*.

Activity

A Declaration—Exclaim It

Purpose: Learn how to make a declaration.

Instructions to child:

Discuss a concern that your child brings up. It could be a school, family or sports situation. Take a few moments to let him see and feel himself in the scenario.

Parent: What do you see in your picture? (Allow plenty of time for him to explore and observe.)

Parent: What do you notice?

Child response: ___ .

Parent: How do you look?

Child response: ___ .

Parent: How does your body feel? (Not just "fine." Give him time to explore and describe any sensations).

Child response: ___ .

Parent: Is there anything in your picture you would like to change? If so, what is it?

Child response: ___ .

Parent: What would you like to change it to?

Child response: ___ .

Parent: Now, how would you like to be in this situation? (You might give him an example of looking stronger or feeling bigger. Allow your child to create his state of how he would like to be).

Child response: I am ___ (strong, big, smart, or whatever he stated)

Parent: Say it again, loud and clear. State it with feeling, like you really mean it.

Child: I am ___ ! (Show him how to use body language to illustrate the power of his words. For instance, raise your hands like you are

continued on next page

a winner, or jump up and down and show how powerful you are. Or put your hand over your heart as you state your declaration).

If your child makes a declaration, but does so in a very uninspiring way, the declaration will not be effective. However, when he makes a declaration that is clear, firm, strong and includes powerful body language, it will move and even encourage him. Tell your child, "Say it like you really mean it!" Don't be surprised if he shouts it out. "That's good!" You can enthusiastically shout it out after he has declared it.

Here are some suggestions for declarations your child might just use. Let him choose his own declaration, however. Note the opposite negative thought which is common when kids are not confident and don't believe in themselves.

Inspired declarations	Negative thoughts
I am a good reader!	I hate to read.
I like myself!	I don't like myself.
I make good choices!	I make dumb choices.
I am a runner!	I'm really slow.
I am a good friend to my friends and family!	No one likes me.
I can do anything I want	I can't ...

Find a time to consistently have your child state his declarations. The two best times are when he just wakes up and when he's ready to go to bed. Be sure you acknowledge your child's declarations. Let's say that your child states a declaration, like "I complete my homework every day." Then everyday he has completed it, make sure you tell him, "Good job! That declaration really works!"

It is important that your child now realizes that he has a new tool in his tool-box. In other words, as he's picturing himself being successful rather than failing, he should know that it is because he's armed with this new tool. And though it might sound corny, it's almost like he's got superpowers. When he uses these skills or powers that he didn't have before, he changes his expectations.

Once your child has created his declarations, have him repeat them consistently day and night, out loud if possible. Your child can increase the effectiveness of the declarations by including all his senses. Have him decorate his room with his declarations, by making signs, pictures and posters that represent his statements. Start including movement with his declarations.

Strengthen Your Declarations

What is so powerful about movement? Simply this: movement is *powerful*. The motor system is critical in the learning process, as noted in Chapter 2, *Your Child's Vision Development*. Remember, vision is learned through a developmental sequence of movement and processing skills, starting in infancy (and in utero). It's through experiential learning, involving multiple senses.

One of the magical places parents and kids discover together is the children's museum which focus on the toddler to eight-year old. Most major cities have one.

These museums have mastered the hands-on motor approach to learning. They allow the children to touch, manipulate and experience what they see, hear and feel. This is how learning is most effective. Here's what you might see and experience. You enter through the museum's doors and you might encounter a flashing fire engine. Kids are dressed in firefighter costumes, hats, and are climbing over and through the engine. They are taught how to make a 911 call and what to say.

Older kids might discover a market place with shelves stacked with goods, checkout stands, even credit card swipers. A kitchen is close by where they can take their goodies and make a pretend meal. Or how about a visit to the vet? They learn about x-rays, positioning of stuffed "injured" animals, how to feed and take care of them, and a little compassion along the way.

The exhibits that are presented in a children's museum focus on developing sensory awareness, social skills, language and gross and fine motor skills. This creates a fun, hands-on learning experience for both parent and child. When multiple senses are involved, learning sticks.

Lost and Found

Have you ever traveled to a specific location over and over again, as a passenger, not the driver? Imagine getting in a car as the passenger. You may or may not pay attention to the landmarks or turns as you are driven to your destination. You get out of the car; not thinking anything more about your travel. Then it's your turn to be the driver. Even though you've been on the route as a passenger dozens of times, there's a difference. It's not the same as actually driving the road, feeling the turns, and seeing the landmarks. You may not be sure what the other driver's route was; what the placement of the landmarks were; or if it was a left or right turn at the intersection. You're a little confused—you know you've been on this road before; you're just not sure how to get where you want to go.

Why did you have problems navigating to your location, especially since you had been there before? Simply this: the actual activity of visualizing where you want to go, and then experiencing the motor movements of seeing the route as you steer, turn, and brake are critical to imprint the total learning experience.

An extreme example of declaration is illustrated by men who were POWs—Prisoners of War. They used visualization and declaration activities that enabled them to survive their horrendous ordeals and maintain their sanity. They did this by working on their golf game! They "saw" themselves preparing for a swing, addressing the ball and following through with their ball landing where their vision directed it. Sometimes, they said out loud their intentions. Many times they had to declare, silently, telling their bodies what to do, as they followed through with their swing—any noise heard by their captors could have lead to further punishment.

The concept of motor experience for learning also applies to developing and utilizing the *See It. Say It. Do It! Model.* Adding motor activities during your child's declarations solidifies the declaration and can enhance results.

Putting It into Practice

Here are two examples of motor strategies to utilize when making declarations. The first is called Lazy 8 Thumb Rotations and the second one is called Cross Marches. They both involve bilateral movement (integration of both sides of the body). Bilateral movements are very important activities to integrate both sides of the brain. There will be additional examples of bilateral movements in Chapter 8, *Learning to Sequence*.

Lazy 8 Thumb Rotations

Cross Marches

Activities

Lazy 8 Thumb Rotations

Purpose: Add bilateral movement to a declaration.

Instructions to parent:

Ask your child to create an image in her mind and a declaration she will say out loud. Have her say it out loud several times. Instruct her to do the following:

Hold both arms straight out, interlock your fingers and place both your thumbs together (show her).

Slowly, trace an imaginary Lazy 8 (sideways figure 8) pattern in the air with your hands.

Keep watching your thumbs as they go around the Lazy 8.

Continue tracing the Lazy 8 in the air.

Now, move your hands and trace the Lazy 8 in the opposite direction.

(Once the Lazy 8 activity is successfully accomplished, tell your child to):

State your declaration while continuing to trace the Lazy 8.

Practice over and over again, until you can easily state your declaration and maintain a smooth Lazy 8.

───── ⚬⚬⚬ ─────

Cross Marches

Instructions to child:

Let's have fun marching around the room.

(Start marching in place.)

Now we're going to add arm movements in a very special way. When your left knee is raised, use your right hand to touch your left knee. When your right knee is raised, use your left hand to touch your right knee.

(Once your child can consistently march with a cross pattern arm movement, then tell her):

State your declaration over and over again as you continue to cross march.

Watch your child carefully through this activity. Many kids lose the cross marching pattern and end up doing what is called a homolateral march. This is where the right hand touches the right knee and the left hand touches the left knee. If that happens, have her stop the activity for a moment and then try again. Take a deep breath. If she can't do it, then work on each piece of the activity separately until she can eventually perform the bilateral integration movement.

Help your child follow this process: visualize a scenario, create a declaration, state it clearly and with power, use movement when saying the declaration, and practice it daily! It will take repetition to integrate the declarations. Eventually you'll see her integrating this process into her daily routines. Work toward eliminating the negative thoughts and building the declarations.

The Chinese, as well as other cultures, have seen the power of declarations for thousands of years. They represent the declarations through symbols and pictures which appear in decorations and paintings.

Dr. H's INSIGHT

In China, silent affirmations (declarations) have been used for thousands of years to help encourage and motivate people. For instance, fish are a sign of upward progress. This is because the ancient Chinese observed fish swimming up rivers and leaping up waterfalls to get to the breeding grounds. Consequently, fish tanks, paintings and ornaments of fish are effective silent affirmations. Today, when a Chinese person sees a fish, he or she immediately envisions upward progress.

We're through the *See It. Say It.* portion of the *Model.* Now, turn the page and let's **Do It!**

Do It!

Words can make a difference. And when words imply action, this can make a dramatic difference in the results.

In 1988, a growing shoe company created advertising history. First, because its new slogan leap frogged market share from 18 percent to 43 percent; second, revenues grew from $877 million to $9.2 billion within 10 years; and third, the slogan became part of the global buzz.

"Just Do It!" is synonymous with attitude and skill. Nike's home run ads rarely focused on the product itself, but on the person wearing the product. The "Just Do It" campaign not only brought in humor, but also captured the philosophy of grit, determination and passion. It was "cool" to just do it.

Nike's slogan and success, and your child have a lot in common.

Does your child have great ideas, dreams, and visualizations, but sits on the sidelines, waiting for everything to be just right, or fearful that he may fail at the task. "It's not the right time," or "Maybe later," he states as his excuse. Have you ever heard those types of comments? Have you ever responded, "Just try it," or "Just do it."

Everyone has fears, some so significant that they stop you in your tracks; and some so minor that you laugh at them when you think back; and some more of a challenge. What are your fears? Heights? Failure or making a mistake? Looking stupid? Not being good enough? Not having friends? Not being loved?

In the children's movie, *Monsters, Inc.*, the viewer is taken behind the scenes of what really goes on in the city of Monstropolis. Sulley, voiced by John Goodman, is the top scarer. The target of his scare tactics is children—children snuggled in their beds who are awakened by a cafeteria of monsters in the middle of the night. Their screams produce the power to run Monstropolis; the employees bottle them for future use.

That changes when Sulley encounters Boo, a little girl who isn't afraid of him, thinking he's a big kitty. Humans and monsters aren't supposed to co-exist in harmony, at least according to the lore of Monstropolis. That, of course, will change by movie's end. After a series of adventures and misadventures, Sulley gets Boo back to her bedroom. She tearfully waves goodbye to him as he steps into the role of CEO and implements a new strategy—laughter will replace fear ... when fear is set aside, the amount of energy produced from laughing is 10 times greater than from fear.

What Fuels Fear

Are you able to manage your fears, or do your fears manage you?

Children also have fears.

Fear can stop your child from taking action. He may be afraid to go out for a sport because he's not very coordinated. Or he may avoid raising his hand in class because he may ask what he thinks is a stupid question and be laughed at.

Be Perfect ...

The drive to be perfect can often interfere with your child's freedom and open-ness to learning. This tendency often shows up with bright, gifted children. These children with perfectionist traits often avoid tasks, or are much slower in completing them due to their fear of making mistakes. They procrastinate about everything. They have very high scores on Intelligence (IQ) testing, except in the areas that require "speed of processing." These kids report that their "brain works faster than their hands and their mouth." In other words, it's like their brain has a very fast, advanced computer chip, but their hands and their mouth are like an old, slow dot matrix printer.

Because of the reduced speed of processing part of the score, the entire IQ score may artificially drop. The reduced IQ score may underestimate a gifted child's potential. These kids often avoid written work since the end product does not come easily. This impacts them in school. They may be advanced in mathematical skills, but because they can't pass the timed math fact test, the teacher won't place them in higher level math classes.

Their frustration factor is huge. There is a disparity in their performance, between their high level thinking abilities and their written performance.

Grades ...

Grades in school may be a great motivator for some kids. However, grades for others may create such pressure that school is no longer about learning; it is about getting good grades and achieving standardized test scores. I've seen many children avoid challenging classes because of the fear of not being able to get an "A" in that class. Therefore, they lose out on what could be an important learning experience, just because of the fear of getting a lower grade. These children actually need to experience failures—and view them as a temporary setback or useful lesson, instead of a catastrophe. They need to find strategies to get through roadblocks. And they need to visualize a different way to move through life.

> Fears create obstacles and often stop us from moving forward in life. These behaviors and avoidances are seen with children of all ages, even with adults.

Let me introduce Joni. You'll see how obstacles created by fear can be removed or modified with the *See It. Say It. Do It! Model.*

Joni's Story

Joni was in the last quarter of her fourth year of optometry school when I met her. She was doing an externship at my office, studying how to examine and treat young children. Joni loved kids and had a very special gift when she worked with them. After several weeks, she still had difficulty completing her vision examinations on my patients. She took too much time, because she kept re-doing tests to make sure she got "perfect" testing results.

One day, I discussed my concern with her. She revealed that this was a very common issue for her. The fear of not being perfect manifested in many other areas of life: school, jobs ... even relationships.

I asked her if she would be willing to spend a few minutes working with me on this issue, utilizing the *See It. Say It. Do It! Model.* She agreed.

I had Joni start with relaxing, breathing and awareness. She immediately noticed how tense her neck and shoulders were. She continued with belly breathing, and then allowed her breath to go into her tight neck and shoulders. She reported that the tightness and tension just started falling away as she continued to relax.

Then I asked her to visualize her very safe, private place; a place where she was comfortable, truly herself, strong and confident. It could be a place she'd been before, or a new place. It really didn't matter. Joni visualized a very beautiful place in nature where the sun was shining bright, and she could smell the flowers. She was relaxed, calm and safe. It was in this safe place that Joni saw herself as strong and confident. She pictured herself standing tall with a huge smile on her face. She saw, felt, and said that she was a powerful, confident woman.

This short 15 minute experience had great impact on Joni. She became aware of how tight her body became under stressful conditions, conditions that she sometimes created. She also realized that she now had a very useful resource of visualizing, through breathing and relaxing (**See It!**). And now she knew that at any time or any place, she could go back to her safe place, a place that she has created where she is empowered and safe.

Joni declared (**Say It!**) her power and became committed to transforming how she approaches her life situations. She knew that she just needed to take several relaxing breaths to get back to her safe place.

At work the next day, she shared with me how impactful the experience had been. She called her mother that evening, and had a discussion regarding some personal issues which had concerned her for quite some time (**Do It!**). Joni revealed that she was very relieved and excited after talking with her mother. I don't know the particulars of Joni's personal issues, and it's not my job as her clinical supervisor to delve into that. My job was to teach and empower her to perform as an excellent optometric clinician. The *See It. Say It. Do It! Model* was the perfect resource in accomplishing that goal.

Joni's work performance at our office greatly improved. Her courage in taking on new tasks and speed in finishing her work was remarkably different from the Joni who first came to my office.

Below is a letter Joni sent me a week after our conversation.

> Thanks so much for taking the time to help me with anti-anxiety/perfectionism techniques. Within one week of the fifteen-minute session, I have seen vast improvements in my self-esteem and level of anxiety. In the past, I have felt extremely anxious and stressed out when I have had to participate in various tasks. Yet, when I use the techniques that I have learned like breathing, visualizing a safe place, and not judging myself and others, the stress level decreases tremendously.
>
> It's amazing how much our own thoughts can impact our day and our perception of ourselves. I know that the results that I have recently experienced are just the beginning of great things to come. The relief I feel today will increase by next week, by next month, and so on, and I am grateful for it!
>
> I sincerely hope that you will continue to help others learn how to better themselves and live happier lives. The world needs more people who are willing to take it upon themselves to help others!

Joni has the tools to take on her challenges through a very different approach. This doesn't mean that she no longer has struggles in certain areas of her life. What has transformed is her approach on how to deal with her issues. Rather than being fearful and stressed, which is how she lived her life, she now comes from a place of power and safety. That 15 minute session was a turning point. She called me months later to report that she continues to use the visualization tools she learned.

As a parent, your child is no different. You will be the primary resource in your child's life—by recognizing what's holding him back and offering an alternative to move him through the blockage.

Get Out of Your Rut

The next two activities give you tools to help you "move out of your rut," literally and figuratively. The first activity is for you, the parent. After you've tried this activity on yourself, then try the second activity. It demonstrates how to take this same process and use it with your child.

Activity
My Car Is Stuck

Purpose: Find a strategy to get out of your rut.

Instructions to you:
Imagine this scenario:
It's 10 degrees in the middle of January, and the snowfall is accumulating quickly. The temperature is falling, the roads begin to freeze, the visibility steadily decreases and you're driving to your child's school to pick her up. Hurry, you're late! Your child is waiting for you.
Was she dressed warmly enough? Will she be able to stay inside the school until you arrive?

You are worried, stressed and are rushing to pick her up. Before you realize it, you've slid off the road into a ditch. You've left your cell phone at home and no one is around to help you.

What do you do? Panic? Get out of the car and start walking? Hope that someone stops to help? Relax and hope for the best? Have you ever been in a similar situation?

Let's get back to our story. Your car is now stuck off the side of the road. The engine roars as you try to build up the momentum to move your car forward. The smell of burning rubber permeates the air as your car wheels spin, but your car just keeps digging a deeper rut.

The visibility is so poor you can hardly see the hood of your car.

What shall you do now? The car just won't move forward.

Stop for a moment and take a breathe.

Allow a picture to form in your mind of all the options you have.

You could choose to stay buried in the snow, and hope someone rescues you.

Instead, how about creating a strategy to move out of the rut? Consider trying something different. Just sit for a few minutes and breathe deeply. Be aware of the tightness and tension in your body. Aha! What if you tried to rock the car backwards to eventually move it forward?

Picture yourself putting the car in reverse. Slowly step on the gas and rock backwards. Then quickly shift to drive and rock forward. Continue visualizing this back and forth motion until you are eventually out of the rut.

State to yourself, "I am a safe driver. I can do this."

Now try it! Good chance that you can eventually rock yourself out of the rut. (Sometimes we have to go backward to move forward!)

What have you done in this activity? You've just gone through the steps of the *See It. Say It. Do It! Model.* You visualized the scenario (**See It**!). You declared who you are (**Say It**!), then you took action (**Do It**!). There is no guarantee that you are out of the rut yet. However, you are not stuck in your thinking anymore. You are looking at possibilities and solutions. This is what is important. How many times have you said to yourself, "If I put my mind to it, I can do anything I want to do." This activity is a strategy on how to "put your mind to it!"

Too often we tell our kids, "Try Harder." What happens? Most likely, the harder they try the worse the situation gets. Next time, you might say, "Try Easier." The less the stress, the more the relaxed state, the better chance of accomplishing the task. Try this next Activity with your child. It is similar to your experience of *My Car is Stuck.*

Activity
Practice Goofing Up!

Purpose: Learn the importance of taking action, through the exploration that there is more than one way to do things.

Take an activity which your child avoids or has a fear of. Let's imagine that your child avoids writing due to his fear of "not writing fast or well enough."

Instructions to child:
Sit comfortably.
Close your eyes and take a few breaths.
(Pause)
Imagine sitting in your class.
Your teacher has just given you a handwriting assignment.
This is a long assignment which will count a lot for your grade in the class.
What do you notice in your mind?
(Pause)

How do you feel?

(*Pause*)

Look and feel any images or body sensations which come up.

Just focus on those body parts and breathe.

Don't make anything right or wrong.

Just notice how you feel and see.

(*Pause*)

Now, let's have some fun!

Imagine that you have many different kinds of writing tools. Big, fat ones. Skinny ones. Markers that sparkle. Paint brushes with bright colors.

Pick any tools you want.

Your assignment now is to see how many different ways you can write.

Write sloppy! Write fast. Slow it down. Make it huge. Make it very tiny.

Be like an artist and just create! Create as many different ways to write as you can.

(*Pause*)

Notice how there are lots of different ways to write. None of them are perfect, they are all just different. None of them are really right, or wrong—they are just different.

Know that next time you have a written assignment, you can choose in your mind as silly or creative writing tool as you want.

Once your child will try an activity that he has avoided or struggled with, have him consider making a declaration as discussed in the previous chapter. Let him create his own. You might hear him say something like:

I CAN do this!

Mistakes and Risks Lead to Success

It's all about taking a risk. Children should be allowed and encouraged to take risks, unless it is a dangerous situation. This also means that your child should be allowed to make mistakes. You can't always save him, nor should you. This is part of the learning process. How will your children learn to make wise decisions if they aren't allowed to learn from their mistakes? It's painful, yes; but necessary.

"Imperfect action is always a winner over perfect inaction," says T. Harv Eker, author of *The Secrets of the Millionaire Mind*. Imagine two students in a race. One is a perfectionist and very fearful because he may not win; this student makes the choice of "perfect inaction" and thereby won't even start the race. The second student runs the race of "imperfect action." This second student will start and finish the race, wanting to win, but not knowing whether or not he will win. Who will win the race? Someone with an imperfect action strategy who will at least attempt to move, or someone with a perfect inaction strategy who won't move because of fear of failure?

As Babe Ruth, the great baseball legend, said, "Never let the fear of striking out get in your way." And James Joyce, an Irish author from the early 1900s said, "Mistakes are the portals of discovery." Praise the efforts of your child, not just the end result. If your child gave his best effort and still struck out, let him know you're still his best supporter with, "You're a tough kid. Way to hang in there!"

Action Plans, Do They Work?

Watch how your child functions. Does he have difficulty completing tasks because of poor organizational skills? Does his desk looks like a disaster? Does he forget where he puts his homework? Is his room a mess? What now?

Successful businesses utilize action plans for their projects. I suspect you've created a form of an action plan in the past week. Do you make a "To Do" list— items that you need to pick up at the store, etc.? Certainly not a detailed action plan, yet one that notes something that needs to be completed. An Action.

Action plans are great organizational tools to follow through on small or enormous projects. Without a plan, accountability and empowerment, an organization has no foundation. In fact, George Brandt, author of *The New Leader 100 Day Action Plan*, states that 40 percent of new businesses fail due to lack of organization and implementation. When specific action plan steps are used, the failure rate drops to 10 percent.[1]

How about modifying this successful action plan strategy to use with your child? When your child builds the skills to plan and organize his activities, his time for work completion and productivity increases. As he becomes more effective and efficient, avoidance behavior and emotional outbursts often are reduced.

Some kids are well organized in all areas of their lives, some are disorganized, and many are at different levels of organizational skills. The goal is to find an organizational system that allows your child to **Do It!**; take action. It's a great habit to start, as it can build a lifetime of organizational skills.

The complexity of the action plan has to be adapted for the age of your child. Older kids now use computerized organizers. For young kids, toys, books, even parts of their closet may be a good starting point. Kids learn early that shoes go on the floor, not in their drawers. How about making a game of putting colors of shoes together or similar types of shoes together (sandals, flip flops are on one part of the closet floor—school and dress-up shoes next to them)? Some schools even implement daily planners.

No matter what your child's preferred learning style is, some type of system needs to be utilized to help your child keep organized. The more creative the system, the better chance it will be utilized by your child. Don't you just create the system—remember, it's for your child, not you (at least directly). Interestingly, if you haven't noted your child's learning style, pay attention. It's going to surface in this process. Consistency in utilizing the organization system is critical to his success.

Putting Action Plans to Work

In the first chapter, I discussed the importance of visualizing the end result and then working backward. Let's say that your child has declared, "I am an excellent student." Have him imagine himself as an excellent student. Let him see what he looks like, and how he feels.

Now what action does he need to take to eventually become a great student? Does he need a tutor? A change in his school schedule? More structured studying time? A quiet place to study? More consistent feedback from his teacher? What?

Discuss all the possibilities with him that will make him a great student. Have him write down in a step-by-step process (or you may if your child is too young) what he needs to do. Add as many dates of completion as possible.

Two of the vision therapists at my office, Beth Fishman-McCaffrey, OTR and Pat Dunnigan, developed a workbook to assist our patients with organization skills. This project was originally initiated to help our patients and parents complete their home vision therapy assignments. The charts worked so well that we adapted them so that they could be utilized in other areas of our patient's lives.

The term action plan sometimes seems to frighten some parents because it seems too overwhelming. We therefore now refer to action plans for kids as organizational charts. This terminology is more accepted by our patients.

The organizational chart for vision therapy may be easily designed as a checklist, or could be more elaborately designed with stickers, pictures or whatever he loves to do artistically. The specific activities on the chart are what you and your child have agreed upon.

If you independently make the chart for your child, don't be surprised if your child doesn't follow the chart very well. Your child needs to own the chart from the very beginning. It starts with his visualization, declaration and then the steps and methods to record accomplishments.

The more fun and creative this process becomes, the more likely your child will use and continue to stay with the plan. If your child becomes bored or stops working on his plan, then a modification to the process is needed. Go back to the original declaration and plan, and then re-create where the organizational chart needs to go now. Rewards for accomplishing steps in the organizational chart are important for most kids. The reward can often be as simple as a hug or complement, a sticker, or a toy he can earn.

Does this work? Absolutely! Even children with significant learning problems will respond to the use of an organizational chart.

Grace's Story

Ten-year-old Grace was diagnosed with learning and behavioral difficulties. She had significant vision, motor and sensory problems and was receiving vision and occupational therapy at my office. Even with all of the complications and difficulties with learning, Grace was able to utilize the *See It. Say It. Do It! Model* with great results.

Grace's parents were frustrated because she wouldn't do her homework. She was unorganized, frustrated, and started refusing to complete any of her chores, besides homework. "It was always a fight, to get her to clean her room, even brush her teeth," her mother would tell us. Excessive time was spent arguing on what needed to be done, with little results.

Her vision therapist discussed these issues with Grace and her mother. All wanted to find an easier way for her to complete her chores. Grace felt like her chores took so much time and were so extensive, that she didn't get to do anything she wanted. She felt she was missing out on play and friend time.

We asked Grace to come up with a list of all her activities required for each part of her day. Once she wrote them down and put a time of completion to them, she saw that she would still have her play and friend time. Her list put closure on the task. She saw that they didn't go on forever.

To the surprise of both Grace and her mother, she actually listed more tasks than her mother deemed important. The two negotiated which were the most important to be completed. For any parent, completion of the daily basic activities for their children without arguments would be a major accomplishment!

Because of Grace's disorganization and learning issues, we decided to simplify the organizational chart. One chart can often be utilized for all activities; morning chores, homework, vision therapy, evening chores ... In her case, we wanted each major daily time session to be a separate chart. A different chart for her vision therapy assignments and homework was also made.

Grace responded very positively and gave feedback as to what should be included in her chart and when those activities should be completed. She really liked being trusted to take responsibility. She asked to be the one to mark off the boxes each day when she completed her task. She loved signing her initials next to each activity, even taking pride as she initialed them.

Take a look at her chart below. She started decorating it with stars and happy faces. It was her own, to create it as she chose. She even complimented herself, "Good Jood" (good job).

Her parents reported the next week that life was much calmer at home. She was very proud of herself and didn't argue about using the organizational chart. It became much easier for her parents to prompt her to do her chores. All they had to say was, "Check your chart." Grace took it from there.

Name: Grace G   **Declaration: I am responsible**

Grace's Morning Tasks   Good JOOd!

Initials	Tasks
ÓO	Put dirty dishes in dishwasher
GO	Brush teeth
	Wash dace
GO	Get dressed
GO	Comb hair
	Throw dirty clothes down the clothes chute
ÓO	Make bed
	Put water in water bottle and put in Backpack
	Put on Shoes.

Grace's Afterschool Tasks

Initials	Tasks
GO	Feed the dog
GO	Do homework
GG	Set table for dinner

Grace's Night Tasks

Initials	Time	Tasks
GG		Put away homework in backpack
GG	→	Choose and put out tomorrow's clothes
GO		Choose snack and put in backpack
GO	8:15	Brush Teeth ← Bath
GO		Wash Face
GG		Throw dirty clothes down the clothes chute
GG		Put on Pajamas
GG	8:30	In Bed

Even with her learning difficulties, Grace was becoming more responsible. Taking ownership of her behavior was critical in the success of using the chart. Several months have passed and Grace's mother reports that she still happily uses the charts and the evening warfare is nonexistent.

Now, here's the bonus: her mother shared a beautiful story regarding Grace's acceptance and use of the organizational charts many months after her vision therapy had ended.

When summer vacation came, a regular babysitter was hired during the times that her mother had to work. The babysitter did what most sitters do—she allowed Grace to watch TV most of the day, even though her mother asked her to do other things: work on math, reading, go to the library, physical activities ... you get the picture.

Grace's mother decided that if the organizational chart was good enough for Grace, it was good enough for the babysitter too! She and the sitter sat together and created one, just as Grace had done. The babysitter loved it and got more involved in the planning and implementation of activities for Grace. Needless to say, Grace's mother was thrilled with the results. Grace has better care; the babysitter is more organized; and everyone is happy. Her mother made it clear that these organizational plans are not just for little kids! Older kids and adults benefit from them as well!

Create Your Own Organizational Chart

Your child's chart should be individualized to meet her daily organizational requirements. Start with the visualization and declaration. Notice that Grace's declaration was, "I am responsible." To be responsible, she and her mother listed all the daily activities for her to be responsible. These would be considered the Goals which are written in Column 1 of the Morning Daily Planner

Column 2 is where your child initials or places a sticker when he completes that goal. Column 3 is for the acknowledgement and "pat on the back." If your child is old enough, have him write a powerful descriptive word like: super job, terrific, amazing, awesome.... If he is younger you can say it to him and then write it and reaffirm it.

Dr. H's INSIGHT

Laminate the chart and use a dry erase marker to mark the "achieved my goal" or "pat on the back" areas. This will allow you to reuse this chart on a day-to-day basis. If you choose to use stickers, make enough copies to last a month so you can have a new sheet for each day.

Sample Organizational Chart

Name: _____

Declaration: _____

Morning Daily Planner

Goal	I achieved my goal (Initials or Sticker)	Pat on the back for achieving my goal
Make bed		
Brush teeth		
Wash face		
Shower or bath		
Get dressed		
Put pajamas away		
Comb hair		
Eat breakfast		
Clean up breakfast dishes		

Name: _____

Declaration: _____

Evening Daily Planner

Goal	I achieved my goal (Initials or Sticker)	Pat on the back for achieving my goal
Homework		
Vision therapy homework		
Set the table		
Eat dinner		
Clean up dinner dishes		
Feed the dog		
Shower or bath		
Put clothes in hamper		
Comb hair		
Brush teeth		
Back pack, homework, shoes, jackets ready for school		
Read a book		
Watch 30 minutes of television		
Lights out at 8:30		

Name: _____

Declaration: _____

School Daily Planner

Goal	I achieved my goal (Initials or Sticker)	Pat on the back for achieving my goal
Homework list		
Due dates		
Materials/supplies to complete assignments		
Backpacks with necessary items, books, worksheets		
Homework check off list		
Organizational chart for daily school work		
Organizational chart for project		

Older kids may be ready for a daily schedule, like your daily planner. Here is an example of such an organizational chart.

Name: _____

Declaration: _____

Daily Schedule

Time	Activity
6:00 a.m.	
7:00 a.m.	
8:00 a.m.	
9:00 a.m.	
10:00 a.m.	
11:00 a.m.	
12:00 p.m.	
1:00 p.m.	
2:00 p.m.	
3:00 p.m.	
4:00 p.m.	
5:00 p.m.	
6:00 p.m.	
7:00 p.m.	
8:00 p.m.	
9:00 p.m.	

The organizational chart is a very effective, simple system to keep kids on track and to self monitor. It builds responsibility, accountability, organization and success. If used consistently, it can become routine and habitual. Eventually, the chart may become unnecessary or different charts may be needed. The key is making it routine and consistent.

Practice, Practice, Practice

Consistency and practice are the key elements for success. Create a schedule for you and your child when homework and chores are done at the same time each day. With parents being so busy, it is difficult to do this. Children thrive with structure and it creates more free time. Without structure, your child may flounder and never get anything done. Then you are back to the frustration, arguing and struggles.

What happens when you consistently practice the *See It. Say It. Do It! Model*? It's transformation time. The Big **Ta-Dah!** On to Chapter 6 ...

6

Ta-Dah!

Why use the *See It. Say It. Do It! Model*? Kids love to visualize and play the activities presented in the first five chapters. But what's the big deal about **Ta-Dah!**? What does this all mean?

Ta-Dah! is the "transformation" part of the VDAT (visualize, declare, action, transform) process. Transformation is about moving or shifting from where you are now to where you would like to be … it is the process of taking continual steps in your life's journey. **Ta-Dah!** It's when goals are accomplished and dreams are realized. There really isn't an end point, for when we accomplish a goal, the excitement of attaining it makes us want to focus on our next goal. **Ta-Dah!** becomes the encourager for all things to come.

The *See It. Say It. Do It! Model* really works. Before exploring this process further with your child, it will be helpful to more fully appreciate how it can benefit you as an individual. The best way for me to guide you is to demonstrate how the model worked for me, and how you might adapt this to your personal circumstances. Without using this process, I don't think I would have ever completed my first marathon; yes, a twenty-six mile race. This was a great opportunity to really experience a **Ta-Dah!** in my life.

Life is a Marathon

I never was interested in jogging. I played sports, but avoided long, endurance, boring activities like running or walking. Walking in nature boosted my spirits, but walking on the treadmill in the winter time was a total waste of time for me.

My daughter started walking long distances as part of the rehabilitation for her back injury. She walked several miles daily, since she could not get back to her more strenuous exercise routine. Eventually those miles turned into a marathon, literally! She walked 26.2 miles, a full marathon. Do you know how long it takes to walk that far? Over seven and a half hours!

I became intrigued with long distance walking after watching her heal. She recommended a hysterical and inspirational book, *Learning to Walk: From a Sofa to a Marathon in Nine Months* by Sheilagh Conklin, an overweight, middle-aged woman who decided on a whim to walk a marathon. She compares her nine-month marathon preparation to her pregnancies, from conception to giving birth to her medal upon completion.

She wasn't well prepared for her first marathon, which took her over nine hours to complete, and left her in total physical and mental exhaustion. Conklin took much more care in preparing for her second marathon 14 months later. She started yoga and learned to breathe and stretch properly. She worked diligently with her dietician, personal trainer, physician, and counselor. As the miles piled up in her second marathon, even though she was physically tired, she revealed that she gained inner strength and felt no pain or discomfort. True to most pregnancies, this "labor" was shorter. She completed her second marathon in less than seven and a half hours.

Rock 'N' Roll!

I wondered if I could take on a challenge that was far beyond my comfort level. My daughter asked me to join her for the Rock 'N' Roll Seattle Marathon. I said, "yes" and then panicked! Only six months to prepare for what I believed to be an impossible goal for me. I mean I can walk, but 26 plus miles all at once might be a stretch even for me.

Registering for the marathon was a declaration in itself—"I'm paying my money to do this!" No coincidence, but this opportunity just happened to arise during the process of writing this book. I literally put the *See It. Say It. Do It! Model* to the test.

Here's my confession—I've never watched a marathon, much less experienced one. I envisioned a marathon as the equivalent of watching grass grow. Boring! I checked out the Internet and found pictures of marathons. I discovered that 25,000 racers were planning to attend the Seattle event that I threw my running shoes into. Breathe Lynn ...

I started to incorporate the steps of the *See It. Say It. Do It! Model*. I printed one of the pictures of the banner at the Marathon finish line; a constant reminder for me. I visualized crossing the finish line on a bright sunny day, with my hands stretched high and a big smile on my face. Remember, in the *See It. Say It. Do It! Model*, you start from the end result (crossing the finish line) and then work backwards.

The picture raised my excitement level for a short time. Then the negative thoughts flooded my mind: "I'm too old. I'm not in shape. My feet hurt. My knee isn't strong. I could never make it ..." The list went on. How would I be able to accomplish such a challenge? I knew little about training for a marathon.

I kept returning to my visualization of me crossing the finish line. "I'm a marathoner," I declared. This was not very easy to state, and I frequently laughed out loud when I said it. Right, I'm a marathoner! I hardly believed it myself. But as I practiced over and over again, I started stating the declaration with more confidence. I even started believing it to be true.

Good enough. The next step was to create a Marathon Action Plan with dates for completion. The steps included buying new running shoes, evaluation at the podiatrist for new orthotics, research on how to train for a marathon, changes in my workout schedule, half-marathon competition one month prior to the marathon, and daily practice of visualizing and declaring, "I am a marathoner."

Marathon day came quickly. We prepared our clothes, snacks and strategy for the race. I had been increasing my physical workouts over the past four months, but hadn't walked more than 14 miles in a day.

I'd love to tell you about the excitement and drama of the start of the race, but we were so far back in the crowd, that it took us 55 minutes to reach the start line. It was a gorgeous day in Seattle; perfect temperature, clear blue skies, and a glorious view of Mount Rainier. The race was on. Around mile eight, my feet hurt. The negative thoughts started filling my mind. "How am I ever going to finish this race? I'm not even one-third of the way and my feet are killing me!"

My visualization of crossing the finish line and declaration kept me moving beyond my pain and discomfort. Hours passed. The struggle continued more in my mind, than my physical body.

Jim Vance, an Elite Coach and a professional triathlete knows about preparing for a challenge. He says,

> The good news is that it's half mental. The bad news is, so is the other half. The athletes who focus on the things they have control over, such as race strategies, nutrition, and warm-ups, are the ones who will almost always perform to their potential, better than their counterparts. The athlete who is focused on things he has no control over, like the weather or other competitors allows doubts and fears to overtake his confidence—perpetuating negative thoughts and making for a long, under-performing day.[1]

We continued past mile 20 and then I hit the wall around mile 22. This is a condition caused by the depletion of glycogen stored in the liver and muscles, which manifests itself by fatigue and loss of energy. In other words, my blood sugar plummeted. I was fatigued mentally and physically. I was unaware of what was happening; I just thought I was getting tired. I felt like my "Rock N' Roll" days were long gone. Luckily, my daughter stayed with me the entire way. She gave me enough sugar snacks to boost my blood sugar level so that I could complete the race.

Crossing the finish line was quite an exhilarating event. Unaware of physical pain or discomfort (maybe I was numb by then), this life challenge became a reality. It really wasn't just about being a marathoner. It was about the process of going beyond what I thought were my physical, mental and emotional limits. It was a test of who I was in the face of challenge, a realization of my true self. It was a huge **Ta-Dah!** for me. Transformation at its best.

Who Is Responsible?

Not everyone will ever compete in a marathon; at least not a physical running race. However, we all run into marathon situations, a metaphor for a demanding, enduring challenge. Working a 14 hour day and then coming home to three screaming kids is what I'd call a marathon. Or what about pulling an all night study session to complete a paper in college? That's a marathon as well. Each of us experience marathons in our lives. The question is, who is responsible for the training and running of your marathon? Who visualizes the task? Who declares it has to be done? Who acts on it for completion? Who usually gets transformed?

You do! If you want to create the life you dream of, then you have to take full responsibility for your life. That means no more excuses, complaining or blaming. Sure, we all have setbacks and blocks. How we deal with these issues is based on our beliefs about ourselves.

As a parent, you are in the unique situation of teaching your child about life's opportunities and challenges. Your child will watch and learn from you. How do you run your marathons? You are his role model for his present and future marathons.

Take a few seconds and just picture yourself in a marathon situation. Do you plan ahead? Do you fully commit? Do you look for excuses? Will you push yourself to continue? Or do you run away? Maybe never even register?

If you become aware of your marathon strategy, you can build on it for more consistent and higher level results. Imagine if you taught your child how to do this at his young age. Look at the life skill you have just given him.

The Breakdown of the *See It. Say It. Do It! Model*

As you utilize the *See It. Say It. Do It! Model,* you may observe some consistent patterns with your child. Perhaps you now notice she is a procrastinator, or she is always in a rush to complete an activity. After decades of working with children, there seems to be three main categories of how children approach their lives:

- She accomplishes what she wants when she commits herself.

- She has great ideas but is frustrated because she stands back and doesn't take action. She doesn't accomplish what she wants to do.

- She works hard, but is getting nowhere, spinning her wheels.

The *See It. Say It. Do It! Model* works well when utilized properly, as demonstrated by the stories in this book.

See It + Say It + Do It = TA-DAH!

What happens when the *See It. Say It. Do It! Model* isn't utilized consistently or thoroughly? These equations demonstrate what happens when all the steps of the *See It. Say It. Do It! Model* aren't completed.

See It – Say It – Do It = **DREAMER**

Visualization without making a declaration or action plan usually results in a dreamer who has not realized his dreams. Do you know a teenager who has always talked about going to college, but just doesn't put in the effort to make good grades? He may have the visualization of going to college but either never makes a strong declaration or takes no action. Excuses are abundant and not much is accomplished. Frustration and/or avoidance of tasks usually increase.

What about the child who works hard just to complete his work, but does not have a special interest, hobby or goal? The equation would look like this:

Do It – See It – Say It = **BUSY WORKER**

Here is a child who just keeps working hard, with no particular direction, just spinning his wheels. Look at the workers who go to work daily, perform the same tedious duties, and then leave work. For some, this may be fulfilling. For others, they may be missing a real passion. Fear often keeps you from having the courage to follow your dreams. Attitudes and situations breed songs like David Allen Cole's *Take This Job and Shove It*.

As a parent, you become the CEO—Chief Encouraging Officer. An important parental duty is to encourage your child to create big dreams. Talk about them frequently. Assist him in finding a way to move towards his dreams.

What if he is a dreamer or busy worker? There could be any number of reasons why he approaches life this way. The reasons could include conditioned behaviors, traumatic experiences, difficult living situations, learning problems, physical problems, vision problems—and many other possibilities. Whether your child is gifted, has special needs, or is just a typical kid, observe him and observe his way of approaching life.

Start implementing the *See It. Say It. Do It! Model* for yourself! Your child will imitate your behaviors. That's a guarantee. If you are a dreamer and don't follow through, then don't be surprised if your child acts the same way. Share your passions and visualizations. Experience the **Ta-Dahs!** together and acknowledge each other. This is the joy of life.

The previous two sections focused on understanding visualization, vision and the *See It. Say It. Do It! Model.* It's now time to address the main area that your child will spend the bulk of his years within ... the classroom. The next chapters provide activities for enhancing development and processing skills to increase academic success.

Part Three

School Readiness & Skills

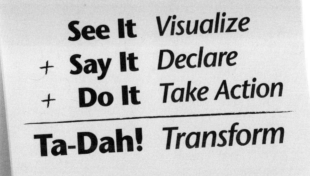

See It — Visualize
+ Say It — Declare
+ Do It — Take Action
———————————————
Ta-Dah! — Transform

7

Why Kids Aren't Ready

What does your child do in his free time? If he is like most kids, he spends hours watching TV and playing video games. A study from the Kaiser Family Foundation in 2005[1] found that the average time that a child watches TV, DVDs and videos is four hours per day. Think about how this might impact your child.

The subject matter and violence seen on TV has been shown to impact the behavior of your child. In addition, TV time takes away from healthy activities like reading, playing with friends, imaginary and creative play, eating dinner together as a family, and participation in extracurricular activities which are important for cognitive, motor and social development. Excessive TV watching has been linked to obesity, behavior and sleep problems. If your child is typical, TV is playing a very big role in his life.

What about video and computer games? Kids find them highly motivating due to their interactive nature. Video games may promote learning, problem solving and help with the development of fine motor skills and coordination.

Research at hospital rehabilitation facilities has shown that some of the Nintendo Wii video game systems, including Guitar Hero, Punch-Out!, Fit, and others, can be used to regain movement and motor skills in physical therapy after a stroke, muscular-skeletal disorders, brain injury and other injuries, because they are motivating and fun.[2]

There are some positive effects from playing video games, but it comes as no surprise that they also can have negative effects. Research has documented negative effects of video games on children's physical and behavioral health.

The American Academy of Child & Adolescent Psychiatry reports that parents should be concerned most about the time that their child plays video games and the content of the games.[3]

Data shows that children become more isolated due to the solitary nature of the game. Spending large amounts of time playing these games can create problems and lead to:

- poor social skills

- time away from family time, school-work, and other hobbies

- lower grades and decrease in reading

- exercising less, and becoming overweight

- aggressive thoughts and behaviors

TV and video games certainly supply fun and are motivating. Sometimes they are over-stimulating. There is little or no movement with most. Players are stationary. There is no social interaction. They often serve as a "babysitter" for kids, with so many parents working and leaving their kids at home and on their own.

Keep in mind that TV and most computer games do not encourage visualization. They feed the child pre-packaged images and in many instances stunt rather than stimulate the imagination.

How long should you allow your child to play video games? Thirty minutes or less per day, after homework has been completed, is more than enough video time. Use these games as a reward for your child's completion of tasks.

Move It!

Sports participation not only provides the opportunity for motor development as well as social interaction, but also gets the kids off the couch and moving. Sometimes these sports teams are too structured, not giving the freedom for creative play. Or they may be so competitive that kids don't get to participate unless they are the super athlete.

When I was a kid, and most likely when you were as well, we didn't have all the video game options, nor as many structured sports opportunities. We played outdoor games: jump rope, jacks, hopscotch, marbles, tether ball, four square, red light/green light and sandlot baseball. These games allowed for creative play. We played until the sun literally set. All these games required creative thinking and eye-hand-body coordination—movement.

Dr. H's INSIGHT

One of the most valuable aspects of sports is the opportunity to build visualization skills. The child observes others, processes the instructions and steps or rules of the game, and then imagines what it would be like to execute the same actions. When ready after this mental rehearsal, the child jumps in and executes the actions according to the motor map she planned. She then gets immediate feedback on how well she did. When visualization becomes a fun part of sports, it helps the feedback process where the child learns and then plans on how to be more successful, or duplicate success the next time around.

If we weren't outdoors, then we were indoors putting together puzzles, doing art projects, or playing board games like checkers, dominoes, scrabble and memory games. Most families had a Monopoly game. These games required visual information processing skills and creative thinking.

The challenge I see as a vision professional is that many kids today are not as active physically. With a lack of physical movement, they miss experiencing integration of vision and movement in real time and space. And, with the time spent on TV and video games, creative thinking activities are reduced.

What kinds of activities can you do to help your child experience the skills which promote healthy, fun and safe learning? Go back to the basics of learning readiness skills. The activities included in this section represent a few of the many excellent developmental movement and visual information processing activities.

Have fun. Allow for free creative play time. Incorporate movement activities. Turn off the TV!

Learning Readiness Skills

Your child learns motor and visualization skills through a series of developmental stages that were identified in Chapter 2, *Your Child's Vision Development*. Also recall that in Chapter 1, *What is Visualization?*, learning style differences were discussed as was the importance of integrating vision with other senses for successful learning and performance.

The Activities in Part III are designed to give your child experiences in sequential, motor, visual information processing and integration skills. Chapter 8, *Learning to Sequence*, is directed towards motor and sequencing activities. Chapter 9, *Developing Visual Information Processing Skills*, focuses on visual information processing skills. Chapters 10 through 14, provide specific strategies for academics such as reading, spelling, creative writing, math, as well as dealing with school stressors such as homework and tests.

And then there is Chapter 15. Are sports and music academic subjects? No, but they are very important in the developmental learning process of children. Therefore, Chapter 15, dedicated to sports and music, is included in this section.

Keep in mind that each Activity in the following chapters can easily be modified for your child. It is essential you find a starting point where the child can developmentally perform.

As your child successfully completes each step of the Activity, increase the demands or difficulty of the task for continued learning. Remember, kids are at different developmental stages, no matter what their age. The Activities included have been modified and used with very young kids, those with learning disabilities, high-level athletes and even advanced students and adults.

Learning to Sequence

Motor Sequencing

Remember the Cross Marches and Lazy 8 Thumb Rotations you learned in Chapter 4, *Say It!?* These types of activities are important in building bilateral integration skills, meaning that both sides of the brain and body are used. These integration skills lay the foundation for higher level processing and movement skills, which were introduced in Chapter 1, *What is Visualization?*

Games such as skipping, hop scotch, and jumping rope are great examples of bilateral movement sequence activities.

This next Activity, "The Creep," requires more advanced bilateral integration skill. Proceed step-by-step through this activity. Kids who are younger than seven and a half may not be able to perform all parts of this Activity, when it comes to naming the left and right. If your child confuses left and right, then more time needs to be spent on understanding the left/right concept.

If your child has difficulty with any level of this Activity, *do not* proceed to the more challenging steps until more practice and success is obtained at the current level. Additional resources for activities to improve bilateral integration, left/right awareness, and motor planning skills are found in Chapters 4, *Say It!*, and 9, *Developing Visual Information Processing*.

Following directions is a sequencing activity. Your child has to understand the directions as to what is to be done first, and then what needs to follow.

Some children will find it easier to respond verbally when you ask for them to repeat the directions. For others, it may be that the physical act of making the movements help them confirm the steps of the sequence.

If your child struggles with sequencing activities, be sure to identify where along the sequence your child is out of step. Then you'll be able to figure out whether the child didn't process what she had to do, or understands the sequence but has difficulty reproducing it.

If the problem is on the intake (she didn't understand it), you will need to go back to fewer or less complicated steps and re-build her confidence before you continue. If the problem is more with the physical movement, then help her make the movement and gradually drop out the support until it becomes more automatic on her part.

Following sequences is a very basic precursor of steps in math and of writing a composition. Sequencing is the first building block used in almost every academic activity.

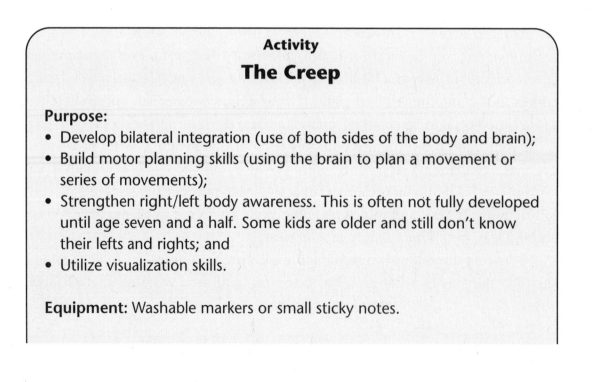

Activity

The Creep

Purpose:
- Develop bilateral integration (use of both sides of the body and brain);
- Build motor planning skills (using the brain to plan a movement or series of movements);
- Strengthen right/left body awareness. This is often not fully developed until age seven and a half. Some kids are older and still don't know their lefts and rights; and
- Utilize visualization skills.

Equipment: Washable markers or small sticky notes.

Instructions to child:

Step 1: Left/Right awareness:

Lay comfortably on the floor on your back.

Raise your right hand.

Great. Now, put it down and raise your left hand.

Good, put it down.

Kick your left leg.

Kick your right leg.

Step 2: Adding visualization and motor planning with left/right awareness.

This time, before you raise your right hand, imagine in your mind that you are raising that hand. Don't raise it yet.

Now, raise your right arm.

> (*Pause,* give your child time to do this.)

Good. Put it down.

Let's do the same with your other arm.

Imagine raising your left arm.

> (*Pause*)

Now raise it.

Good. Put it down.

(Do this for each arm and leg.)

Step 3: Adding more demands to left/right awareness.

Now, move your left and right arm at the same time.

Good. Stop moving your arms and move your left and right leg.

Great, stop moving.

(Do additional combination of limb movements.)

Step 4: Motor planning with more challenging demands.

Now, before you move, imagine moving the body parts I tell you in your mind before you actually move them.

Visualize moving your right arm and your left leg.

(Give him time to visualize the movement before he does it.)

continued on next page

Now move both at the same time.
Stop.
Visualize moving your left arm and right leg.
Now move them at the same time.
Great.
(Continue giving him two or three limb movements, always having him
    visualize before the movement.)

Step 5: More abstract visualization and motor planning.
(Draw an "R" with a marker or use a sticker on the back of your child's
    right hand and right knee, and an "L" on the back of his left hand
    and left knee.)
Close your eyes.
Pretend that you are watching a movie of yourself on your hands and knees.
Describe what you look like in the picture in your mind.
(Example of your child's response: "I see myself on my hands and knees
    outside on the ground. I'm wearing my jeans and t-shirt.)

Now, visualize yourself creeping on your hands and knees moving first
   (touch the "R" arm).
And then this (then touch the "L" arm).
Then this (Touch the "R" leg).
Then this (touch "L" leg).
Now, describe what you see and how you are moving.
(Wait for his response).
Great, now move in that pattern, repeating right and then left, just as
   you imagined the motion.

Observe what sequence of limbs he moves. Did he move the correct
pattern in the correct sequence? R arm, L arm, R leg, L leg. If he
followed that sequence, there is a good chance that he pictured the
pattern in his mind. It is important that during the visualization phase,
do not verbally say the words: right, left, arm, or leg. Let him visualize
the movement just with your touching his limb and without the
auditory clue of left or right.

Use a different pattern each week. For example:
   Week 1 – R arm, L arm, R leg, L leg
   Week 2 – R arm, R leg, L arm, L leg
   Week 3 – R arm and R leg together, L arm and L leg together
   Week 4 – R arm and L leg together, L arm and R leg together

If your child performs the incorrect movement pattern, stop him and
ask him to picture it in his mind one more time. Repeat the process,
touching the arm or leg in the correct order. Encourage his observations
and ask what he is seeing or noticing.

Step 6: Adding visual fixations to any step of the Activity.
This time, whenever I say to move your right arm, look at the R on your
   hand when you visualize and actually move.

continued on next page

Same thing when I say left arm, look at the L on your hand.
Also look at the R or L on your knee when I give you those limbs.
(Always start by having him visualize himself on the ground. Ask him
    what he notices and feels.)

You and your child can create variations and more challenging games as
he completes each of the steps of "The Creep".

Confused with Left/Right
If this entire left/right creep sequence is too challenging, especially with
your younger child, then start the activity sequence without using the
terminology of left/right. Reduce the number of commands—maybe
just one arm or one leg. Here is an example of how you might modify
this activity:

Parent: Lay on the floor, on your back, with your eyes closed.
    "See" yourself in your mind.
    Feel the floor and notice any sensations.
    (Touch one part of his body, like his left arm, and say):
    Raise the part of the body I just touched.

Continue to touch other body parts, one at a time, and have him raise
    that part.
Eventually start touching more than one body part simultaneously (like
    the right arm, left leg).
See if he can process more than one touch stimulation at a time.

If he has a problem remembering the sequence of the movement you've
    created, have him make a movie in his mind of the movement
    pattern, rather than trying to remember each command.
Increase and decrease the demands of the task depending on his
    response. After he demonstrates success on this part, continue to
    make this game more challenging.

Auditory Sequencing

Does this scenario sound familiar:

Parent: Go upstairs, pick up your clothes and brush your teeth.
   (Your child goes upstairs and forgets what to do; gets lost in the
   sequence of commands and doesn't complete the task.)
Parent (yelling one command at a time): You're not paying attention!
   Now, go upstairs! ... Pick up your clothes! ...

Was your child not paying attention, or unable to follow the sequence of verbal commands? It's difficult to know without more information, as there are many causes for attention problems, including sensory motor and visual problems. If your child shows significant problems with concentration and focus, then it would be appropriate to have him evaluated for attention problems through his pediatrician or family doctor, school and/ or psychologist/psychiatrist.

Not all kids need medication for attention problems. Some can learn behavior management techniques; some improve with vision or occupational therapy; some may do better with better nutritional support; and some might gain benefit with medications. No matter the treatment, wouldn't it be helpful to have strategies to improve his sequential processing? The next three Activities are just for that!

Creating a task chart is helpful when your child has difficulty with the sequencing of commands. He can either draw pictures or cut out pictures from magazines representing all the tasks he needs to do for a certain time. Have him arrange the pictures in the appropriate order. Make sure the pictures are fun, colorful and meaningful for him. Now you just have one command to give: "Go check your chart!"

Activity

Following Directions

Purpose: Strategy to remember a sequence of tasks or commands.

Instructions to child:
Picture yourself in your mind.
Describe what you look like.

(Pause)

Imagine yourself going upstairs, picking up your clothes and brushing your teeth. (Create a two or three step command.)

(Pause)

Now, *visualize* watching yourself going upstairs, picking up your clothes and brushing your teeth.

(Pause)

Make a movie of what you just did in your mind of you flowing from one task to another.

(Pause)

Play the movie again in your mind.

(Pause)

Have fun and run the movie backwards!

(Pause)

Watch your movie one more time.

(Pause)

Now open your eyes and actually go up stairs and follow the movie in your mind.
Great job!

Here's a fun Activity that you can play almost anywhere; in the car, at home or on the playground.

Activity

Going On a Picnic

Purpose: Building visual memory, sequencing, and visualization skills. Describe what you will bring to a picnic. Say each object in alphabetical order, A through Z, and repeat the entire list as you add your next item.

Instructions to child:

Parent: I'm going on a picnic, and I'm bringing an *a*pple.

Child: I'm going on a picnic and I'm bringing an *a*pple and a *b*anana.

Parent: I'm going on a picnic and I'm bringing an *a*pple, *b*anana and *c*hocolate.

Child: I'm going on a picnic and I'm bringing an *a*pple, *b*anana, *c*hocolate, and *d*onut.

Parent: I'm going on a picnic and I'm bringing an *a*pple, *b*anana, *c*hocolate, *d*onut, and an *e*lephant.

Child: And so on… Continue as far down the alphabet as you can.

You can also change the destination. You can say, "I'm going on a trip to the park or zoo or any other destination that your child is familiar with."

Activity
Bunny Hunt

Purpose: Adding movement to a sequential, visualization activity. Make it fun and creative with actions and sound effects. The parent will be the leader of this Activity, with the child following and adding sound effects when prompted. After completion, you should encourage her to be the leader.

Instructions to child:
Pretend that you are going to catch a bunny (or your favorite animal).
Let's start walking close to the ground so we can find one.
(Get on your hands and knees and start crawling around.)
Hey, there are a bunch of different trails here. Remember them because we have to go back through them on the way home.
Say (together), we're going to catch a big one! Come on, let's have fun.
Boy, this door is heavy (pretend to open your house door).
Open the door—*Creakkk*, and close the door behind us, *Clunk* (sound of door closing).
We're walking along ...
Wow, there's some tall grass! Go through the grass—*Swoosh, swoosh*. (Brush hands together as you say swoosh, swoosh.)
Walking along ... I see some mud. Go through the mud. (Make some nasty noises here. Boys always seem to love this!)
Walking along ... There is a bridge. Go over the bridge—*Clip clop* (or click your tongue as you knock your knuckles together).
Walking along ... Oh no! There's more water. Can't go over it. Can't go around it.
Guess we'll just swim through it—*Swim, Swim* (stroke your arms like you are swimming).
Brrrrr! Get out of the water and shake off—*Shake, shake* (shake whole body).

Walking along …

Let's climb that tree and look around—Climb, climb (with arms climbing).

Look around. I see a cave right there (hand on forehead and turn head like you are looking).

Climb down the tree (arms and legs climbing down).

Sneak quietly over to the cave—shhhh. (Tap hands quiet on knees.)

Ah! There's a bunny! Run! (Everything goes fast now like you are running away.)

Run, run.

Up the tree (climb up).

Down the tree (climb down).

Run, Run. Swim through the water (stroke your arms like you are swimming).

Clip clop, clip clop, over the bridge.

Run through the mud (nasty sounds).

Run, run. Through the grass. Swoosh, swoosh.

Almost home. Run, run.

Here we are … Open the door (creak); close the door (clunk).

Whew! We are safe! (Big hug.)

Want to play again? Now it's your time to take me on a trip somewhere!

Source: Paul Hulet

Take a few seconds before initiating other games and activities by asking your child to first visualize and plan the movement in his mind before starting the movement. Great athletes use this strategy over and over again!

You've noticed that the Activities have physical, mental and verbal parts. Unless your child is developmentally challenged, she will employ each as she learns sequencing, a critical component to her learning and confidence quotient.

Along with sequencing skills, your child will develop the visual information processing skills identified in the next chapter, both critical in building a solid academic platform for your child.

9

Developing Visual Information Processing Skills

$\mathbf{I}$ remember the first time my daughter read a book. It brought tears to my eyes. What a miracle, to watch her grow, develop and eventually learn to read. How did it happen? In several years she went from a dependent infant, to an independent learner. She learned to talk, explore her world, play with games and puzzles, identify shapes and forms, and now she's reading. How she did it was most likely the way your child does: step by step. There were many developmental steps she had to master for this "miracle" to happen. Chapter 10, *Reading Opens a Whole New World*, explains the reading process in detail.

The Model of Vision, outlined in Chapter 2, *Your Child's Vision Development*, defines visual information processing (VIP) as,

> Understanding what we see, where things are in space,
> integration of visual information with other senses,
> eye-hand-body coordination, visual memory, and *visualization*.

This chapter is devoted to learning and experiencing the development of your child's VIP skills.

Remember when your child was a toddler and worked with simple jigsaw puzzles? You gave him different-shaped pieces. He turned them every which way, trying to figure out how each piece fit in the puzzle. At pre-school age, he could put 10–20 puzzle pieces together.

This ability demonstrates one of many VIP skills that lay the foundation for the essential academic skills of reading, spelling, writing and math. If a child has not experienced or has difficulty with these basic VIP skills, he will often struggle academically.

Miscommunication

Communicating directions clearly and effectively leads to good visualization and vice versa; good visualization leads to clear communication. Have there been times when you think you were clear (**See It!**) and articulate (**Say It!**) in communicating with your child, and were dumfounded with the end results (**Do It!**)? What happened? Did you miscommunicate? Did he misunderstand or not listen? Maybe, a little of both.

Your responsibility as the communicator is to use language that the receiver clearly understands. Otherwise, you'll end up with communication snafus.

Take the making of a peanut butter and jelly sandwich. Ask your child how to make one. What do you think you'd get?

Activity

Peanut Butter and Jelly Sandwich

Purpose: Learn how to communicate exactly what you mean (match your language to the visualization in your mind).

Materials needed: Peanut butter jar, jelly and slices of bread.

Instructions to child:

Parent: Tell me how you make a peanut butter and jelly sandwich? What's the first thing you do?

(Be sure to *exactly* follow his instructions to you. For instance, if he says,)

Child: Put the peanut butter on the bread.

(He hasn't given you enough information to do it correctly! So make this point by literally putting the jar of peanut butter on the slices of the bread.)

Child: Hey, that's not what I said.

Parent: Oh really, please tell me again what I need to do.

(Again proceed exactly as he tells you. Don't tell him what he needs to say. Let him work at improving the language he uses to guide your visualization and ultimate response.)

Parent: Now, what's next?

(Continue with making the sandwich until you are done. See if it looks the way your child intended.)

(Next, let's change roles. You tell him how to make the sandwich and let him follow your directions. Purposely say silly things like …)

Parent: Take a scoop of the peanut butter out of the jar and spread it around.

(You didn't tell him to use a knife, and he might just stick his hand in the jar and take out some peanut butter. Be prepared for a mess!)

Have fun! Silly, but very effective.

This Activity can be hazardous to your kitchen. The laughing and silliness that comes from this game is rewarding in itself.

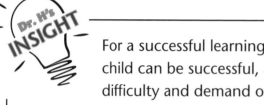

For a successful learning experience, always start where your child can be successful, and then gradually increase the difficulty and demand of the activity.

When vision integrates with language, a whole new world opens. The next Activities have the feel of a puzzle or game. Don't underestimate them. Even adults can feel challenged. They are very powerful tools to build VIP skills.

Never Underestimate a Block

Parquetry Blocks are multi-colored and have different geometric shapes. Some have patterns to use with them as well. The Parquetry Blocks are frequently used in pre-school and kindergarten classrooms and are designed to build VIP skills. But, did you know that these Parquetry Blocks Activities are also used by some National League Football teams to evaluate the VIP skills of potential draftees?

As with all the other Activities in this book, it is not about the end result of obtaining the "right" answer, but it is about the learning process; making errors, learning from the experience, developing strategies, and integrating with other senses.

Parquetry Blocks Activities

Source: Developed by Dr. Harry Wachs and adapted by Dr. Robert Sanet and Linda Sanet, COVT.

Overview: The following Parquetry Blocks Activities are designed to develop VIP skills starting from concrete steps of duplicating block-block patterns, to more abstract processing demands of turning and rotating block designs. Activities include understanding shapes, forms, visual memory, visual-spatial, and visualization abilities. Verbal communication also plays a very important role in these Activities as well, both in describing the task and listening to the communication.

Materials needed: Set of Parquetry Blocks (obtainable at most teacher supply stores), opaque paper or cardboard to hide your blocks, transparent plastic sheets (from office supply store), and double-sided tape. Use the double-sided tape to stick the block patterns on the transparent sheet.

Set-up:
Sit next to your child at a table.

Spread out all the blocks in the set on the table so that you and your child can reach them. (Some sets have 32 blocks, so that you have plenty to work with.) Make sure that you and your child have identical sets of blocks in color and shape.

Parquetry Blocks Activity

Block to Block

Purpose: This is a basic shape-matching activity that serves as the basis for higher level processing.

Instructions to parent:
Build a simple design using just two blocks initially on your plastic sheet. Use the double sided tape to keep blocks on the plastic sheet when you move the sheet. Show it to your child.

Parent: Use your blocks to make a design exactly like mine.
  (Your child duplicates your design. Check his design by placing your
    plastic sheet with your block pattern on top of his newly formed design.)
Parent: Is your design exactly like mine?
          (Wait for your child's response.)

continued on next page

Parent   **Child**

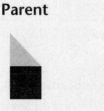

Parent: If not, can you tell me how your design is different from mine?
(Wait for your child's response. Enabling the child to discover what it is that makes his design different is the basis for a child being able to self-critique his performance rather than being fed answers.)

Parent: How can you change your design to make it look exactly like mine?
(Wait for your child's response.)

Parent: Ok, now you build a design for me to copy.
(Child builds a design.)

Child: Copy my design.
(Parent purposely makes an error to see if your child sees the error.)

Parent: Did I do this ok?

Child: (Observes and then says) No, this isn't right.
(Parent makes the correction.)

Child: There, that's better.

(*Pause*)

(Continue taking turns in making a pattern for each other, and then checking each other's for accuracy.)

To increase difficulty:

Increase the numbers of blocks.

Leave space between some of the blocks, instead of always touching all sides of the block with another block.

To decrease difficulty:

Use fewer blocks.

Place blocks exactly side by side.

Parquetry Blocks Activity
Visual Memory

Purpose: Increase visual memory skills.

Instructions to parent:
Build a two to three block to block design behind a barrier where your child cannot see the pattern. A piece of paper or cardboard works well.
Remove the barrier for 10 seconds and let him look at the design.
Do not allow him to pick up shapes while he is viewing the design.
Now cover your design and ask him to make the pattern that you did, from memory with his blocks.

To increase difficulty:
Increase the numbers of blocks.
Leave space between some of the blocks, instead of always touching all sides of the block with another block.
Decrease the time to view block designs.
Talk to your child or distract him when he's viewing the design.
Have him recite the ABC's or count while viewing the pattern. This keeps him from verbally describing the process, and encourages him to use his visual memory.

To decrease difficulty:
Use fewer blocks.
Simplify the design.
Give your child a longer time to view the block design.
Eliminate all distractions.

When your child is able to visualize a design and reproduce it with ease, he is ready to enhance his visual manipulation skills.

The next two Activities work on visual manipulation.

Parquetry Blocks Activity
Visual Manipulation—Flips

Purpose: Increase visualization flexibility.

Instructions to parent:
Using the double-sided tape, build a two or three block design on your transparent plastic sheet. Say to your child:

Parent: Build your design the way it would look if my design is flipped. Visualize flipping the pattern in your head before you start to build. (Specify flipping to the left, right, up, or down.)

Flips—Side to Side

Parent	Child

Flips—Top to Bottom

Parent	Child

Let him build his design as it would appear if flipped. When he thinks he's made it accurately, take your plastic sheet with your design and flip it according to your command. Then place it on top of his design to see if it matches his pattern. Have him check his design for accuracy. Remove your design and place it back on the table in its original position.

Parent: Now, build your design the way it would look when flipped top to bottom.

Have him check his design for accuracy. Continue on with more complex designs if he is accurate. If not, simplify the designs until he is successful with the Activity.

Parquetry Blocks Activity

Rotations

Purpose: Increase visualization flexibility.

Instructions to parent:

Before you start, orient your child to what a whole, quarter, half, and three quarters of a circle looks like. This can be done simply by showing an example design. Be sure he understands what it means to turn the design the specified amount.

Quarter 90° | Half 180° | Three Quarters 270° | Whole 360°

Build a two or three block-to-block design. Say to your child:

Parent: Build your design the way it would look when rotated one quarter turn (90 degrees) to the right.

Parent

Child

continued on next page

Do not allow him to copy your design and then rotate his pattern one quarter turn. Have him start from scratch, rotate it in his mind, and then lay it out the way it's supposed to be finished. Have him do this several times at the one quarter turn rotation, using several blocks. Be specific as to whether he should do the rotation either to the right or left. Check it and have him make corrections, just like he did with the flip patterns.

Parent: Now rotate your block pattern three-quarters turn to the right.

Parent	**Child**

This requires manipulation of the design image in your mind.

To increase difficulty:
Add additional shapes and rotations.
Show him a design, covering the design and having him make
   the rotated design by memory.

To decrease difficulty:
Use fewer blocks.
Simplify rotations.

The next Activity will develop your child's ability to follow and give verbal instructions while visualizing the description of the design.

Parquetry Blocks Activity

Build and Describe

Purpose: Improve visualization-verbalization skills. This is critical for communication.

Instructions to parent:

You need a barrier for this part.

Build a two or three block-to-block design behind a barrier. A piece of paper or cardboard works well.

Do *not* show your design to your child.

Verbally describe the pattern using the descriptions shown in the illustrations that are at the end of this Activity.

Here's an example of a Build-and-Describe Activity:

Parent: Hold your red square so that it looks like a square.

Place the red square in the center of your transparent sheet.

Now pick up your yellow triangle.

Hold it with the right side up and the long side down, facing the bottom of paper.

Then place it so the center of the long side of the triangle touches and aligns with the center of the top side of the red square.

Now pick up your blue diamond, hold it so that the short points are up and down. Place the top left side of your blue diamond so that it touches the bottom side of the red square.

Your child then needs to listen to the description, visualize and then make the design from the verbal information as you describe it. Once completed, the patterns are viewed and checked.

Now, reverse the Activity. Let your child make a design and have him describe it to you. Make your pattern specifically from his directions. This Activity emphasizes the importance of accurate visual processing and verbal description.

continued on next page

Watch your child's breathing, as he may get stressed.
Always acknowledge steps of achievement and completion. Once he gets the hang of it, this becomes a fun game. Don't be surprised if he can do this better than you!

Verbal Commands

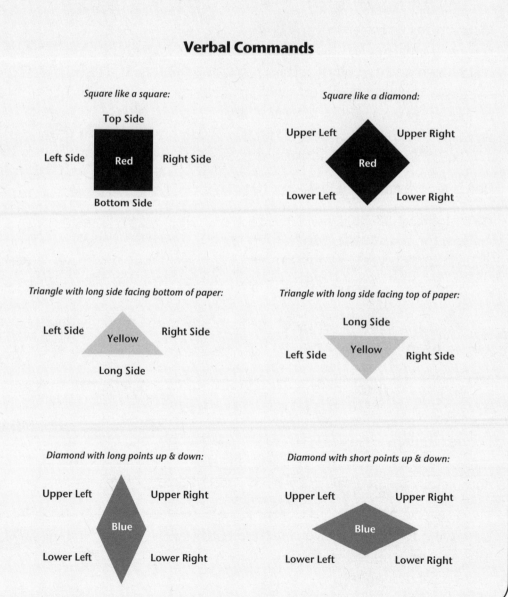

Square like a square:

Top Side

Left Side   Red   Right Side

Bottom Side

Square like a diamond:

Upper Left   Upper Right

Red

Lower Left   Lower Right

Triangle with long side facing bottom of paper:

Left Side   Yellow   Right Side

Long Side

Triangle with long side facing top of paper:

Long Side

Left Side   Yellow   Right Side

Diamond with long points up & down:

Upper Left   Upper Right

Blue

Lower Left   Lower Right

Diamond with short points up & down:

Upper Left   Upper Right

Blue

Lower Left   Lower Right

Communication is critical—words, tone, and inflection. If you become frustrated because your child doesn't "get it," consider changing your descriptors and modifying your language and tone. You may need to simplify the Activity. Always work at a level where your child succeeds. Otherwise, one or both of you will end up frustrated or angry. And probably with a few tears.

Let's get back to the NFL players. Why would the Parquetry Blocks be used with professional athletes? It's all about visual perception. The skills derived from successfully performing the Parquetry Blocks Activities can be likened to seeing the "whole field" from different perspectives. It doesn't matter what position they play, players need the ability to analyze, process and anticipate where a player or the ball may be—whether they are on your team or the other team. Being adept at VIP gives the advantage of seeing and responding to situations more quickly and successfully.

Verbally describing the Peanut Butter and Jelly Activity and using the Build and Describe Activity focus on the skills needed to articulate clearly what you visualize in your mind. Too often you and your child will end up giving each other mixed messages, each believing that communications were clear. Unfortunately, the clarity may only be on the sender's side and not the receiver's. When communications get mixed, it becomes apparent that one or both of you either don't have a good picture in your mind of what you want to say and/or you need to practice your verbal or listening skills. The integration of language and visualization is one of the key skills for reading.

Reading Opens a Whole New World

Reading is a very complex task that requires a number of skills such as decoding (breaking down the words), sight word recognition (seeing a word and immediately knowing the word) and comprehension (understanding what the story is about). Some educators feel strongly that reading is totally a language-based activity and that vision is not related to reading. My response to them is, "OK, then cover your eyes and read!"

Sometimes educators don't seem to see the humor or logic in my response. Their narrow, myopic viewpoint to the actual process of reading may lead to an incorrect diagnosis of the problem. Take Natalie, a typical nine year-old, whose mother said,

> Natalie is so smart, in everything, but school. Her teacher told
> me that she just needs to practice her reading more. But she
> hates to read! She loves me to read to her, but she seems so
> unmotivated to read herself.

Sound familiar? Or, is your child at the other end of the spectrum—an avid reader, devouring every book she can get her hands on?

What are some of the key elements to becoming a good reader? How do you encourage and move your child from a poor reader to one whose attitude is, "Bring me more?" Since reading is necessary for almost every other class in school, it is a priority to master.

Visualization and Language

Reading involves integration of visual and language systems. In *Visualizing and Verbalizing for Language Comprehension and Thinking,* author Nanci Bell states:

> Visualizing is an answer as to how we process language and thought. The brain "sees" in order to store and process information. Both thinking and language comprehension are founded in imagery. Visualization is directly related to language comprehension, language expression and critical thinking. Imagery is a primary sensory connection in the brain . . . I make movies when I read.[1]

The success of reading is dependent on implementing consistent educational reading programs. There are many different philosophies as to how and which reading program is the best. My concern is that your child receive a reading program that fits his learning style; and as long as he is reading successfully. If he isn't, then he should be evaluated by a reading specialist to determine what he needs: a different type of reading program, tutoring, or a developmental vision evaluation for VIP difficulties.

What can you do at home to enhance your child's reading experience? Help him learn to love why reading can be so much fun! Make it "movie" time when it's reading time.

Steps to Making Movies When You Read

You can help your child in his quest to be a great reader by implementing the following steps:

- Model the visualization strategy for your child.

- Allow your child to create his own visualizations and share them with others.

- Integrate visualization into daily activities.

Modeling Starts at Infancy

Read to your child, even as an infant. When you read to your baby, you start her off on the visualization track. How? Every time you read, you reinforce a variety of concepts that every reader uses. Your baby will see you turn pages and read text from left to right. Babies and young children start with picture books, and parents point to the pictures on the page, usually starting on the left side, moving to the right. They learn speech patterns and sounds. When your baby becomes a toddler, she will hold her own books and imitate what you do. First babbling, and then forming real words. Pointing to the pictures, looking left to right. Ultimately, she learns to read fluently and comprehends the story as though it were a movie in her mind.

Kids love to be read to. Ask your child to close her eyes and to listen carefully to what is happening in the story. Read a short passage and then stop. Share with her what you imagined when you read the passage; what the characters looked like, what they were doing, what else you saw. Then, ask her what she saw.

Talk to her about "making movies" in her mind as you read to her.

Use descriptive books, full of imagery, such as Maurice Sendak's delightful book, *Where the Wild Things Are,*

> That very night in Max's room, a forest grew and grew and grew until his ceiling hung with vines and the walls became the world all around.

When you read that one sentence, what do you see? What kind of pictures popped up in your head? What do you think your child might imagine?

Depending on the ages of your children, choose an appropriate level story that provides excellent descriptive passages. Books that you might read in addition to those already mentioned throughout this book include the *Magic Tree House* series by Mary Pope Osborne, Dr. Seuss books by Theodor Seuss Geisel, Danny Schnitzlein's *The Monster Who Ate My Peas,* Roald Dahl's *Charlie and the Chocolate Factory, The Diary of a Wimpy Kid* series by Jeff Kinney or J.K. Rowling's *Harry Potter* series.

The good news is that there are terrific and imaginative books published every year, just waiting to be discovered by you and your child. A great resource is the children's librarian at your nearest public library, or the one at your child's school. Don't forget to ask your child's teacher for recommendations as well.

Allow Your Child to Practice

Read a short passage of a very descriptive book and frequently pause. Instead of you sharing your "movie," ask your child specific questions about his movie. "What do you see in your movie? What do the people look like? How do you feel? What do you hear? And so forth.

Let's look at author J.K. Rowling's words from *Harry Potter and the Sorcerer's Stone* when Harry first discovers Diagon Alley:

> "Three up ... two across ..." he muttered. "Right", stand back, Harry.
>
> He tapped the wall three times with the point of his umbrella.
>
> The brick he had touched quivered—it wriggled—in the middle, a small hole appeared—it grew wider and wider—a second later they were facing an archway large enough even for Hagrid, an archway onto a cobbled street that twisted and turned out of sight.
>
> "Welcome," said Hagrid, "to Diagon Alley."
>
> He grinned at Harry's amazement.[2]

It's your child's turn. Have her create her own mental images with the Harry Potter piece above. She creates the ability to visualize the book herself—filling in the pictures that the author has created using only words.

The ability to generate visual images from texts becomes increasingly important as she moves from richly illustrated storybooks into "chapter books" with relatively few pictures.

When you read to your child, you model with words, with your tone, with the way you deliver your phrases. Your child's antennae hears and receives. She imitates. In her mind, she begins to create images. She imagines herself in the scene. Her movie.

Encourage creativity and building awareness. Be sure to acknowledge that her movie may be different than yours. There is no right or wrong, just a difference.

Integrate Visualization into Everyday Learning

As your child further understands the concept of visualization, make it a part of daily activity. This book is designed to give you experiences and ideas on how to make visualization a habitual part of your life. The dozens of Activities suggested throughout reinforce the key and critical elements of successful learning. Each has been designed and used hundreds, and sometimes thousands, of times by children and adults alike.

I Don't See Movies in My Head

Although the goal is to develop great comprehension in reading, just asking a child to "visualize what you read" or "make a movie" may not work if the child has difficulty with basic sensory processing skills. As discussed in the Chapters 8, *Learning to Sequence* and 9, *Developing Visual Information Processing Skills,* the steps to improve sensory processing include motor development and VIP. These are critical skills in developing the foundation for higher-level visualization.

Once the building blocks are in place for visualization, encourage your child to write stories that integrate the pictorial language with written language. We'll explore this more in Chapter 12, *Creative Writing Can Lead to Anywhere.*

The process of developing reading comprehension starts from imaging pictures, and then proceeds to word imaging, sentence imaging, sentence interpretation, paragraph imaging, and then eventually reading comprehension. If your child is struggling in this developmental process, additional reading tutoring, language therapy, and/or vision therapy may be necessary.

Is Reading Out Loud the Same as Reading Silently?

It is sometimes painful to listen to a child read out loud. With a slow, halting voice, and little expression, he sounds out word by word. By the time he completes the sentence, it's hard to remember what he just read! How do you know what his silent reading is like? The answer may surprise you.

Many advanced readers struggle in school because their teachers hold them back in reading if their oral reading is not fluent. They often are very strong visual learners, prefer silent reading and do well silently, as tested on reading fluency computerized programs such as the Visagraph Eye Movement Recording System.[3]

Dr. Linda Silverman is a psychologist and director of the Institute for the Study of Advanced Development, and its subsidiary, the Gifted Development Center, in Denver, Colorado. She has very specific recommendations for reading techniques for Visual Spatial Learners in her book, *Upside Brilliance—The Visual Spatial Learner.* She writes:

> Ask these bright kids comprehension questions and they often
> can easily answer them. They may need some help with
> symbol imagery strategies and possibly visual tracking skills.
> But understand that their learning style may be different and
> they should not be punished in reading because of that.[4]

Reading orally is a much different process than reading silently, involving a different eye movement, tracking and cognitive process.

Improving Reading Fluency

- *Good visual efficiency skills* (refer to Chapter 2, *Your Child's Visual Development*). Some kids use their finger to track along the line. This is common with early readers and usually phases out in second grade. If he still needs it after second grade, then this is a sign of a possible vision problem which needs to be evaluated by a developmental optometrist.

- *Needs to know all the words on the page.* If he is decoding words as he reads, there is no way can he read smoothly, nor comprehends easily. Automaticity of recognizing words rapidly is a key to fluent reading.

- *Read an easy book together.* You read while your child follows along in the book, so that he can hear smooth, fluent reading.

- *Learn to read by phrasing or reading several words at once.*

- *Play games where you time him reading a short passage.* Have him keep track of his time. Then have him read it again and see if he can beat that speed.

- *Allow your child to read silently for at least five minutes per day, any book that he knows all the words in.* He can even re-read the same books. This gives him practice in the eye movement fluency when he doesn't have to struggle with words.

- When your child has to read out loud, have him pretend that he is an actor. Have him read the story like he's on the stage, speaking to Grandma in the last row. This often helps with the anxiety and fear around reading. Telling a smart kid to "slow down" when he reads usually results in frustration and avoidance. But telling him to shine as a brilliant actor, gives him a new place to start from.

- *Be in a safe environment.* It's important that your child can take a "risk" on reading out loud without embarrassment.

Dr. H's INSIGHT

They'll Laugh at Me. I Must Be Stupid!

Jenny is an eight-year-old third grade student who not only struggled in reading but also constantly degraded herself, "I'm a terrible reader," she would tell her family and friends.

She was referred to my office for a developmental vision evaluation. Jenny struggled with reading, even though she had been in tutoring for months. The developmental vision evaluation revealed visual skills and VIP deficits. Glasses were prescribed for focusing problems and then she started vision therapy. She showed excellent improvement throughout the vision therapy and her reading improved.

Even with her improvements in reading, Jenny still thought of herself as being a "terrible" reader. She dreaded reading time at school.

The *See It. Say It. Do It! Model* was utilized throughout her vision therapy. After teaching her to relax and breathe, we asked Jenny about her visualization of what it was like when it was her turn to read in class. She reported seeing herself very small in a dark room with many larger children surrounding her. She saw and heard the other students laughing at her and calling her "stupid," if she made a mistake when reading aloud. No wonder she was a reluctant school reader—what kid wants her classmates to laugh at her and call her stupid? None!

This demonstrates the power of visualization, whether it be positive or negative. Jenny's negative visualization fueled her fears. Her fears created a road block to reading.

We asked her how she would like to change her visualization to help her feel safer and stronger. She imagined herself being larger and did this by "blowing" herself up, like blowing up a balloon (**See It!**). She started smiling and her body posture became more upright, as she pictured herself physically larger and more powerful. We asked her how the classroom looked in her visualization. She reported that the room automatically became lighter, the other students shrunk down in size. Her classmates stopped laughing at her.

Jenny was now empowered and very excited about reading. Her job was to picture herself as she did in practice, coming from a larger, powerful place.

She really had fun moving through the classroom as a powerful student. She declared, "I'm the biggest person in my classroom. I'm a strong reader" (**Say It!**). The stress of reading aloud faded. She practiced seeing this visualization, especially before it was time for her to read (**Do It!**). She was excited about how much better she could now read in class.

At the end of vision therapy, our patients often write their "success story" acknowledging how vision therapy impacted their lives. Here is part of Jenny's success story, in her words:

How My Life Has Changed

My life was getting harder and harder as I was going to higher grades. I started having trouble when I was in 2nd grade. In 3rd grade I had a tutor, but it really didn't help much. But then I came to Vision Therapy. I got new glasses that helped me a lot. I used to see words as big blobs on a paper, but now I see them as real words! Then I had to go to vision therapy and what a success that was! I went from the smallest person in my classroom to the biggest. In other words, I used to be afraid to read in front of the class but now I feel more strong to do that. My mom says, (and she quotes her mom) "I feel Jenny has become more confident in reading and writing."

Jenny demonstrates the power of the *See It. Say It. Do It! Model*. Her reading problem involved visual efficiency and VIP skills, as well as confidence. She experienced and greatly acknowledged her transformation into a strong reader. Jenny's outcome is the perfect example of a **Ta-Dah!**

Albert Einstein sums it up well, "If I can't picture it, I can't understand it." He certainly knew the power of visualization, and now, so do you! Wait until you learn how easy and fun it is to use visualization in spelling. On to the next chapter ...

11

Acing Spelling

Spend a little time in a second or third grade classroom and take a look at the written work from some of the students. Notice how some kids spell words accurately and some spell poorly? Look at the papers with misspellings. Most likely, you know what the word is because the student has spelled it phonetically; in other words, she spelled it the way she heard it—not the way she sees it.

Schools call this "creative spelling" or "phonetic spelling." In the early grades, it is encouraged because students have a larger vocabulary than ability to spell. When your child has a written assignment, you want her to be creative and descriptive. She uses words that she knows but does not know how to spell them. That is appropriate. Eventually, you hope she learns to spell more words and that those types of errors are seen less frequently.

In the movie, *Akeelah and the Bee*, 11-year-old Akeelah Anderson is an ace speller. She's taunted by classmates who call her a "Brainiac" because she is smart. Akeelah's love of spelling comes from her father—he loved words. Before his death when she was six, they would play word games daily. Instead of hanging with her friends after school, she now plays computer scrabble games, she maintains journals with columns of words she memorizes every day, and she reads the dictionary like it was a comic book late into the night.

She's bright, skips school, yet shows up to take the weekly spelling test that she consistently gets 100 percent on. Frustrated, her teacher gets her to sign up for the first school spelling bee instead of being sent to the principal for her truancies. Naturally, she wins.

Her teacher and principal want her to participate in the spelling State Championship—the first time the school will ever have an entrant. Akeelah is resistant. She doesn't want to be singled out, whether it's positive or negative. Reluctantly, she finally agrees. The principal recruits a friend, who just happens to be a previous Scripps National Spelling Champion, to be her coach. Resistance again surfaces, "I don't need any spelling coach," she tells anyone within hearing range.

"The best spellers in the world have coaches," responded Laurence Fishburne as Dr. Joshua Larabee, Akeelah's new coach. He sets up a series of activities and exercises—some visual, some sequential, and some integrative play. In one scene, he notices that Akeelah taps the side of her leg with her hand and fingers, as she recalls the letters of the words. He excitedly refers to it as her "trick," a physical thing that will trigger an answer for her. Her trick is a rhythmic movement that she has created unconsciously to recall the needed answer. He then sets up a series of exercises involving passing basketballs and jump roping while she recites and memorizes new words.

Kids often have "tricks" to trigger their recall of information that is used in school, just as Akeelah did. Her gift was that she was a great speller. Her coach uncovered how to take her to the next level—the Nationals where she becomes co-champion, as only Hollywood could make it happen!

Creating a Great Speller

What if you don't have an Akeelah, but you have a child that you "know" can do better in spelling than what he is currently doing? What can you do if your child needs some help in spelling and how do you do it? In the previous chapter, I identified a number of learning, processing and developmental issues that can impact all studies, including spelling. There may be a genetic component as well.

Spelling problems may stem from a multitude of difficulties including:

- Poor visual memory;

- Inadequate development of symbol imagery;

- Deficient sequencing skills;

- Lack of integration of imagery and language; and or

- Inappropriate utilization of visualization strategy.

Does your child practice day after day at the kitchen table, verbally spelling her words accurately? Then she goes to school and bombs the spelling test. She may see the word in her mind and accurately spell it out loud, but she seems to lose the words when she writes them. This is not uncommon. Some kids have visual motor (eye-hand) problems; when they go to write the word, they often use a different strategy and write the way they *hear* the word, not *see* the word. It's as if they're rehearsing lines for a play. In some instances they're able to play back the tape and write the words correctly for a spelling test, but can't spell the word correctly in a different context because that's not the way they memorized it. They have the spelling of the word in isolation but really don't have a picture of what that word looks like in their head.

That is why I refer to the spelling strategy as *see it-write it*. Make sure the motor system is involved. Several chapters, specifically Chapter 2, *Your Child's Vision Development*, Chapter 4, *Say It!* and Chapter 8, *Learning to Sequence*, emphasize incorporating motor and movement skills into learning.

It is very important to make sure that your child studies spelling using motor and movement skills. Don't make it a chore. Just make sure there is some type of motor response practiced.

This next Activity is a great way for your child to learn to spell. Initially, it may seem to take time to go through all the steps with each spelling word. As soon as your child gets the process, then it becomes automatic. Practice until it becomes a habit.

Activity

Spelling
See It, Then Write It

Purpose: Become a great speller.
Equipment: Colored markers and index cards or strips of paper.

Instructions to child:

Sit comfortably in your chair. Take one of your spelling words and write it
   on this card using whatever color marker you would like. Make it big
   and colorful. You can use as many markers as you would like.
(Child writes word.)
Great! I'll take the card from you.
(Hold the card up at your child's eye level and an arm's distance away
   from her face.)
Pretend you have a camera. With your "camera," take a picture of the
   word in your mind.
(Take the card away.)
Now, with your eyes open or closed, tell me about your picture. Describe
   the color of the letters, the size, the texture (rough, smooth),
   brightness (dull, shiny).
(Pause, wait for a response from your child.)
Raise your hand like it is a larger marker (or a magic wand or laser sword,
   or whatever your creative child would like to use).
While seeing the word in your mind, trace the letters of the word in the
   air with your hand (or wand or sword).

Tips:

Have fun with this. Allow her to make the letters big, little, fat, skinny.
Have your child write the words on a whiteboard, chalkboard, large
piece of paper, or even in the sand. Have her pretend she's a musical
conductor and she *conducts* by spelling the letters with her magic
baton—or a princess with a magic wand or a Jedi with a laser sword;

just make sure there is some type of motor response practiced. Some kids learn to spell when they are jumping on a trampoline, saying a letter of the word with each bounce. The goal is to keep her interested, involved, and successful in the process.

If your child has difficulty seeing a picture, try the following:
Show her the card again.
Try holding the card further from her face. Sometimes moving it away gives her more space to see the card. Weird thought, but try it.
Break the word into smaller groups of (2 to 4) letters. And then show the card again. For example, visualize the word TRANSFORMERS. If she can picture the entire word, great! If not, then break the word up into smaller chunks like:

Trans

Form

Ers

If she still has difficulty seeing any letters, ask her:
What do you notice about the picture in your head? (She may not see a word, but maybe a picture or an object. That's fine.) Ask her about the object. Keep questioning her on what she notices, just to get her used to being aware of the pictures in her mind. If she seems stuck here, then you may need to go back to the Parquetry Blocks in Chapter 9, *Developing Visual Information Processing Skills*, and work through the steps to build visualization.

Once your child reports seeing the word, say:
Write the word on a board or paper as you *see* it. See if it *feels* right to you.

Spell It Backward!
When your child has the spelling strategy down, she can spell it forward or backward. It's just reading the letters off the picture in her mind. To verify that she really sees the word and just doesn't memorize it, ask her to spell it backward.

continued on next page

Say to child:
See the picture of the word in your mind. Spell the word backward.

Listen to the smoothness of her voice. It will help you know if she can
    see it. If she can't see it, you will hear her say a few letters from the
    ·end, then stop and pause, as she tries to go back and forth to
    figure out the word. Stop the process if you notice this. Go back
    to flashing the card and seeing the letters.
Remind her to look up if she is stuck on a word.

Parents have expressed concerns, "What if my child spells all her words
backward at school?" I reassure them, that if she knows the words well
enough to spell them all backward, she won't have a problem.

If you still think you have a problem after she uses this Activity, I'll
personally talk to the teacher if she spells backward. In over 30 years
of practice, I've never had to talk to a teacher about this issue.

Activity
Explore the Size and Shapes of Words and Letters

Purpose: All words have shapes and sizes. This activity builds more awareness as to the visual aspect of a word.

Say to child:
Note the difference in the sizes of these letters of the alphabet. Write them out, using lowercase letters.

"short" = a, c, e, i, m, n, o, r, s, u, v, w, x, z
"tall" = b, d, f, h, k, l, t
"long" = g, j, p, q, y
"capital" letters, like in your name, are "tall."

Say the letters of the word by their size, not the actual letter. For example:

The word "road" would be = short, short, short, tall.
The word "pony" would be = long, short, short, long
The word "yard" would be = long, short, short, tall

Take a card and write a word on it. Go through the visualization process with your child as explained previously. This time, instead of spelling the word by the letter names, spell it by their size.

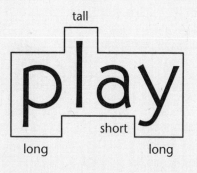

continued on next page

More Spelling Games

Choose a category such as colors, and ask:

Parent: What color is spelled with 3 letters and is spelled short, short, tall?
Child: red.
Parent: What color is spelled with 4 letters and is tall, tall, short, short?
Child: blue.

Other categories to explore and play the same size spelling game include animals, food, transportation, something in the car, a television show, a verb, a noun ... Anything else you can imagine!

Try a variation of the above game. Now substitute with animal shapes.
    Think of animals that have extreme body parts.
        "Tall letters"—giraffe, dinosaur, and flamingo
        "Long letters"—monkey, possum, mouse
        "Short letters"—cat, bird, owl, turtle, fish, ant

Say an animal representing the size of each letter in the word. Such as:
        The word "road" would be = cat, bird, owl, giraffe
        The word "pony" would be = monkey, turtle, fish, mouse
        The word "yard" would be = possum, bird, ant, dinosaur

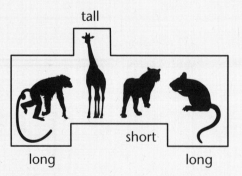

These kinds of games can be fun, open up the imagination, can be played anywhere, and makes them think! And, makes you think too.

Obstacles

When I started using the visualization strategy for spelling with my patients, I used to be very specific as to what I would tell a child to visualize. I would ask him to "see a chalkboard in your head" so he could "write" the word on the chalkboard. I learned very quickly the importance of giving open-ended suggestions. Here is what happened with one of my patients:

Dr. H: See a chalkboard in your mind.
Child: I don't see a chalkboard, it's not working.
Dr. H: What do you see?
Child: A helicopter.

(At first I was surprised with this response, but then I recalled that in all the helicopter movies I'd seen, the pilot had a clipboard of some sort. I asked him):
Dr. H: Does your helicopter have a pilot.
Child: Yes.
Dr. H: Hmm. Next to the pilot, are there any papers or a clipboard on the seat?
Child: Yeah, a clipboard.
Dr. H: Great, is it okay to use the clipboard to write the words on them?
Child: Sure.

Then we continued on through the spelling strategy, writing the words on the imaginary pilot's clipboard.

Observe and listen to your child. Let your child guide you to guide him.

Children are always full of surprises. I worked with a very bright six-year-old child who wasn't reading or spelling well. He was advanced in his verbal language, but both the teacher and parent were concerned about his reading and spelling. IQ testing placed him in the gifted range; however basic developmental motor and visual efficiency problems were present. These problems interfered with his ability to learn easily. He could visualize well, but only with pictures, not letters or words.

This child attended vision therapy and worked very well throughout the first two months of therapy. At his first vision therapy progress evaluation, I asked him how things were going in school. His four-year-old brother, piped up, "He's doing great now that he is using the visualization process for spelling!" (Wouldn't you know, his brother was also gifted?)

Once your child learns to spell the word, have her visualize herself as a great speller, going through the awareness of all senses **(See It!)**. Then ask her to make and state a strong declaration like "I am an awesome speller," or whatever she comes up with **(Say It!)**. Have her create a plan of how and when she will practice her spelling **(Do It!)**.

Here is a great success story written by Nicole, a second grader (seven-year old) after completing vision therapy. I'm including her *exact* words and spelling. Nicole's words,

> The changes I have noticed since I started vishon therapy are meny. First I have much neater handwriting. Now I can tell my left from my right. My cursive is a lot better. Now with leter spelling vishualization, my memory and abilitity to take a mind picture have improved. With the help of Tootie Toss (a bean bag pitch game), my eye hand coordination is superb! Vishon therapy has really helped me.

For a seven-year old, her writing ability is impressive. Chalk it up to another successful experience implementing the *See It. Say It. Do It! Model*. Nicole's writing sample paves the way for Chapter 12 *Creative Writing Can Lead to Anywhere!*

12

Creative Writing
Can Lead to Anywhere

Quinlan, a five-year-old kindergarten student, loves her teacher to read stories to the class. One morning, her teacher read a story from the *Think! Draw! Write! Workbook,* by Jean Marzollo & Katherine Martin-Widmer. This workbook contains activities to help children learn creative thinking, self-expression, and writing skills. The lesson was all about magic sneakers; where would you go if you had magic sneakers? You could go anywhere you want. Where would that be?

The students were told to imagine they had a pair of magic sneakers. They were instructed to make a picture of where their magic sneakers took them, and then to write about their picture. Quinlan chose to go to Pokémon® World where Japanese characters, seen in cartoons, games, movies and collector cards live.

Quinlan drew her picture of the main three Pokémon characters that were in Pokémon World when she visited with her magic sneakers.

Quinlan described her picture (shown on the next page) to the class, saying,

I could see Pokémon (bottom right corner of the picture) in my mind so it was easy to draw. I couldn't see the other two animals in my mind (upper right and lower left), so I couldn't draw them very well.

Her teacher reported that her Pokémon drawn character looked most similar to the real Pokémon, as compared to the other characters she drew; the ones she couldn't see but knew belonged in the picture. The scan of Quinlan's picture is black and white in this book. But in Quinlan's world, the colors she used were red, yellow and blue—all vividly done. Quinlan's sneakers and shirt are red, her pants are blue, Pokémon is yellow, and his friends, Diamond and Pearl, are yellow and red. (I learned who they were when I saw an actual picture.)

Draw yourself in these magic sneakers. Then write a story about where you will go in them.

Creative writing is anything where the purpose is to express thoughts, feelings and emotions rather than to simply convey information. This picture is creative writing! Even five-year olds utilize visualization skills.

Most five-year-olds don't spell accurately. Quinlan completed her assignment when she wrote about her picture, "Poceman Wrot" (translates to "Pokémon World.") Everyone knew, and saw, exactly what she saw.

I Have No Ideas for My Story

"I don't know what to write about." Have you ever heard this comment when your child has been given an assignment to write a story? What usually happens next? The response parents commonly hear is the, "I don't know how/what ..." The frustration builds, the avoidance of task predominates, and not much gets written.

Young children use the creative writing process easily. As kids get older, they seem to forget to use the creative writing process and jump right into writing words. When there is no picture, there are few ideas. This is a process your child needs to continue to develop and strengthen his skills for writing proficiency. Your older child may not physically draw his picture on paper any more, but should do so in his mind.

This next Activity gives your child experience writing a story from the picture he creates in his mind.

Activity
Write About Your Pictures

Purpose: Learn how to write stories.

Instructions to parent:
Read a very descriptive story, full of imagery, to your child. Refer to Chapter 10, *Reading Opens a Whole New World,* for book resources or pull a favorite from your child's bookshelf. If you are looking for "new" material, a visit to the children's section of the local public library is an excellent starting point.

Instructions to child:
Parent: Draw a picture about the story I just read to you.
   (Encourage her to include as much detail as possible in her
      picture.)
   (Ask questions about her picture to help reflect on her story.)
   (This is the first step of *write about your pictures.*)
Parent: This is fun (or awesome, fantastic, great—use the words that
      are comfortable for praise and acknowledgement)!
   Tell me about your picture.
Child: This is …
Parent: I love it! Now, write a few sentences describing your picture.
   (If your child knows how to write.)

Use the language: "Write about your pictures." This helps your child tap into his creative sense and visualization.

When my daughter was six, she proudly brought home her latest paper from school. Take a look at Becky's creative writing sample:

As a first grader, Becky drew a picture about her family and then wrote her story:

"Me Faml is Pa no a Fsw."

Let me translate: My family is playing on a Ferris wheel.

Some parents would be concerned with the misspellings, letter reversals and sequencing in Becky's writing. At this age, don't be worried. Be happy that your child is writing and creating. Becky's picture is happy, she and the family are having a great time; look at their smiles.

She doesn't know how to spell many words, but her picture is worth a thousand. At this point in her development, it's about building the foundation and confidence for creative writing.

You'll be surprised how much more your child will write when you give him the instruction, "Write about your picture," instead of just saying, "Write a story."

I tried this writing strategy with a classroom of severely learning disabled students. The teacher asked them to write about their houses. Basically, their stories didn't say much more than, "Here is my house."

Then the teacher asked her students to draw a picture of their house. The pictures they created were far more than just a big house. There were trees, flowers, windows, puppies ... everything they could picture about their house. Then the kids were told to, "Write about their pictures." The teacher was shocked at how much more detail was written in their stories.

It's Writing Time

When your child is writing a story, don't be concerned with the actual hand-writing, spacing or sizing of letters, punctuation, grammar, or spelling. Encourage him to focus on the picture in his mind and let all the details and description just flow out of his hand. Later, he can edit or check his paper. Yes, I know, kids and adults hate to edit—the attitude is usually "I'm done." However, if you push a kid to write neatly with accurate punctuation, he usually either forgets what he wants to write, or purposely only writes short sentences to avoid the writing process. The goal is to let the information flow out of his head onto the paper; write, write, write! Editing comes after the piece is created.

Many kids avoid handwriting activities. This can be due to a number of reasons including:

- Poor eye-hand coordination

- Fear of not expressing himself well or making errors

- Frustration

- Laziness

There are two factors which impact your child's successful completion of any activity. One is the skill. Does your child have the developmental ability to actually write? And the second factor is his "perception of the skill." How does your child perceive the task? "It takes too long. I hate it. I write so sloppy ..."

Some kids are so frustrated or fearful of the task, that their perception of the task is worse than the actual performance of the task itself. They often stop before they even start the task. This is where visualization can come in to help them change the picture in their mind.

Creative Writing Tips

All writers have tips, tricks, and techniques to get them started, just as Akeelah did as she recalled her spelling words. Here are several that I've learned from my young patients and colleagues:

- Visualize yourself successfully completing the task.

- If you get stuck in thought progression of the story, gently remind yourself to **review** your pictures.

- Audiotape a story, listen to it, create your picture, and then write it.

- Encourage young writers to use their own words that create pictures in their mind—this is when writing really sparkles!

- Start with short stories.

- Fear and criticism often create writing blocks—brainstorm! Visualize!

- Be silly. Have fun!

Drawing Your Thoughts

Some kids won't start writing because they are overwhelmed by too many ideas at once. They don't know how to organize their ideas or use a traditional outline. One of the best ways I've found to get through this obstacle is to have your child use a mind mapping strategy to organize his ideas. A mind map is a diagram used to represent words, ideas, tasks, or other items linked to and arranged around a central key word or idea. It is a great way to take notes, problem solve, and organize thoughts.

Think of the mind map as a tree (shown on the next page). The *trunk* represents the *main idea*. The *branches* are the *main subdivisions of facts* about the main idea. These branches may be representing characters, setting or location of story. The *leaves* provide *further detail* about each category. If there are *roots*, they could be *references and research*.

Let me take you through a mind map. The writing assignment for this child was to write a story about boats.

The *trunk of the tree* contains the main subject, "boats."

The *branches* are lines drawn from the *trunk.* They represent the type of boat, such as fun, military, sports, rescue, transport, and service.

The *leaves* are then drawn from the branches illustrating examples of each type of boat, including speed, fishing and sail in the fun category.

This next activity demonstrates how to create a mind map. Your child can use words or pictures (drawn or cut from a magazine) to create his mind map.

Mind maps are fun, creative tools to tap into your child's visualization that enables him to organize ideas without getting stopped by the structure of grammar, neatness, spelling and accuracy. They are especially good for visual-spatial types of kids whose thoughts bounce from one idea to another, without an organized or sequential pattern.

Activity
Creative Writing Exercise: Mind Mapping

Purpose: Helps with organizing ideas or thoughts for creative writing.

Instructions to child:
Draw a tree trunk in the center of your page.
Use any color marker or pen for the trunk.
Write a main word or idea of what your story is about in the trunk.
Draw the branches from the top of the trunk representing topics or facts of your main idea.
Label each branch line with a topic or fact.
Draw leaves off of each branch for more information.
Use colors to organize your mind map. Consider using one color for each branch and its leaves; then another color for another branch and its leaves.
Let your ideas flow out and plug them into whether is appropriate on your mind map.
Once you've completed your mind map, sit back and look at it. See if you need to move or reorganize any of it.
Make your changes.
Now, it's story time. Write what your mind map is about.

Move through Your Writer's Block

Creative writing is a complex task which involves visualization, organization of thought, and the motor output of expression. Difficulty with handwriting can sometimes be a factor with your child's creative writing process. If your child struggles with handwriting, encourage fine motor activities including drawing, painting, cutting and other eye-hand coordination games. If significant delays in handwriting are present, then an evaluation by an occupational therapist or developmental optometrist may be appropriate to help improve fine and gross motor skills.

If your child avoids creative writing because of handwriting issues, here are some recommendations that may be useful for him:

- Have him tell you his story and you write it down for him. That way he can share his thoughts without being frustrated with the handwriting process. Then have him write the final copy from your notes.

- Cursive writing is often easier and more successful for children. The flow and movement of the letters in cursive, rather than the herky jerky/stop/go movement in printing, is often more fun and easier for many kids.

- Word processing can greatly reduce the frustration of editing and recopying. I encourage kids in 4th grade to start learning keyboarding skills so they are good at keyboarding by 6th grade.

Remember the two factors which impact every activity mentioned earlier in the chapter? The first one is the actual skill or ability and the second is the child's perception of the skill.

Joey's Journey

Joey was a bright second-grade student who struggled in school. He had vision and visual motor problems, including three eye muscle surgeries for crossed eyes. He wore bifocal lenses for farsightedness and focusing problems. For Joey, handwriting wasn't fun. It was difficult, almost painful for him to undertake.

His handwriting was sloppy and not well spaced, as seen in the first sample below. The top sentence represents what Joey was to copy. The lower sentence is Joey's writing, Pre-Vision Therapy.

As you can see in the Pre-Vision Therapy sample below, seven-year-old Joey is having a difficult time. And no wonder, he hated writing and avoided any task requiring it. We discontinued the test at five minutes, even though he had not completed the sentence.

Joey came to vision therapy every week and was consistent in doing his home vision therapy activities. The therapy emphasized improving his visual efficiency and VIP skills. Things changed for him after six months of vision therapy. All visual skills improved, which improved his ability to read and write. At the end of his therapy, what I saw was a happier kid who no longer avoided writing.

Look at the sentence in the Post-Vision Therapy sample copied by Joey after completing his vision therapy. Note the improvement in his letter formation, spacing, legibility, and speed of completion. It took him less than four minutes to complete the sentence. You can see his handwriting skill improved.

**Handwriting
Pre-Vision Therapy**

**Handwriting
Post-Vision Therapy**

Joey's perception of his writing dramatically changed as well. In his words,

> My writer was crammed in me and squished. Now it's gotten
> much bigger and I can write better.

Even the youngest of children can write. Some will write with their words and some with pictures. Either way, *think of the core as always starting with the picture in the mind,* even in tackling challenging subjects, such as our next chapter on math.

13

Math Can Be Fun

Some kids do well at math, some don't. Those kids who struggle in math do so for a number of reasons:

- Can't remember math facts.

- Does poorly on timed math tests.

- Does well unless he has to read instructions or do story problems.

- Doesn't understand the concept of time or money.

- Does well except makes errors because he misaligns columns and numbers due to poor handwriting or a visual problem.

- Inverts numbers.

- Can't understand the basics of shape, size, or form.

- They believe it's too hard.

What is math? According to the Wikipedia found on the Internet:

The study of the measurement, properties, and relationships of quantities, using numbers and symbols. Through the use of abstraction and logical reasoning, mathematics evolved from counting, calculation, measurement, and the systematic study of the shapes and motions of physical objects. Today, mathematics is used throughout the world as an essential tool in many fields, including natural science, engineering, medicine, and the social sciences.[1]

This chapter is not about theoretical and high level mathematics. Rather, it's designed to give you and your child strategies to learn basic math concepts and math facts.

Math Problems?

Let's look at a couple scenarios of why your child might struggle with math. It's important to understand where the breakdown is, as solutions are different for each scenario.

Concepts

If your child struggles with the basic concepts of math: understanding shape, size, form, time, money or space (fractions and percentages are a form of space), then there may be a developmental visual information processing problem. Activities in Chapters 8, *Learning to Sequence* and 9, *Developing Visual Information Processing Skills,* may be beneficial to build your child's foundation skills. Additional math tutoring or vision therapy may also be necessary for more involved students.

Kids who usually do well with concepts are those who love puzzles, Legos®, card games, and other visual spatial types of activities.

Calculation

Some kids make silly mistakes, like adding instead of subtracting, or misaligning columns so that wrong numbers are added. This could be indicative of visual problems (not seeing small detail well), visual motor problems (poor eye-hand coordination), or impulsivity (he just goes too fast).

Using graph paper, or turning a piece of notebook paper sideways, can assist them. It creates vertical lines to keep their columns organized when calculating with columns, like 46928 + 345, in my example below. If this doesn't help over time, they may have a visual problem.

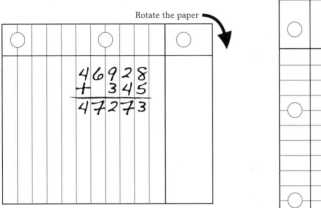

Rotate the paper

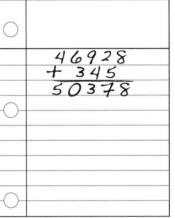

NOTE:
Wrong columns added results in the incorrect answer.

It's Backwards

Some kids invert their numbers or write them in the wrong order, for example, 32 for 23. If your child is under eight, it may be considered developmentally normal. If she is older than eight, directionality, not knowing her left from right, or sequencing may be an issue.

Make sure your child has a thorough vision evaluation to determine if there are visual efficiency or visual information processing problems. In addition, academic testing from your school may be necessary.

Story Problems or Directions

If your child can do the math, but gets lost in the reading of directions or story problems, then this is really not a math problem; it is a reading problem. Math word problems present a special challenge in being able to visualize what the writer had in mind. Then your child must convert that picture into the math operation/equation necessary to solve the problem. Work with the teacher to make sure your child isn't being penalized in math because of the reading. Read the directions or story problem to him, and then let him do the math. In the meantime, he needs to get help for his reading problem. See Chapter 10, *Reading Opens a Whole New World* for more information on reading.

Math Facts

Memorizing math facts is a challenge for many. I bet you can remember memorizing the dreaded multiplication tables in elementary school. Some kids can easily memorize math facts, but can't pass the timed math tests that teachers give routinely. If you think it is just a matter of speed of completion, then ask the teacher for more time on the test or give your child a fewer number of math problems. Have the teacher check to see if your child knows his facts orally, as some kids can tell you the answers much easier than writing them down. Processing speed can be aided by flash card practice. Have addition, subtraction, multiplication and division sets, and decrease the exposure time necessary for your child to come up with the answer. This helps increase automaticity of the math facts, which enables speed.

Does any of this sound familiar? Remember the discussion in Chapter 11, *Acing Spelling,* on writing spelling words? It's a similar problem of difficulty with motor output. Your child shouldn't be penalized in math because of slower handwriting or processing speed.

What if he struggles to recall the basic math facts? Then the exposure time of the flash cards isn't the limiting factor in processing speed. The problem is in understanding how to arrive at the answer, or in memory.

The next Activity can be used to memorize facts in all four basic operations: addition, subtraction, multiplication and division. It relies on visualization and a similar concept as the Spelling Visualization strategy: see it, then write it. The key is creating the picture to write from!

Activity

Math-Fact Strategy

Purpose: Learn a visualization strategy to remember math facts.

Materials: Index cards, markers

Instructions to child:

Give your child the index cards and markers and tell her:

Parent: Draw a triangle of a math fact. 7 x 8 = 56. Put 56 on the top
point and 7 and 8 will be on the bottom corners. Use any colored
marker you'd like. Make the triangle and numbers big! Any numbers
will work. The top number is the product of multiplying the two
bottom numbers. (For example if you had 24 at the top, the bottom
two numbers would be 6 and 4 or 8 and 3).

Also note where the signs for the functions are (x for multiplication,
÷ for division).

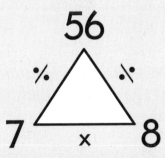

(Once your child has drawn the math fact, take the card from her. Hold
the "triangle" card out and slightly above her eye level.) Say to her:

Parent: Pretend you have a camera. Take a picture of the triangle and
numbers in your mind. Trace it with your eyes.

(Pause)

continued on next page

Parent: Now, describe the card the way it looks.

           (Pause, let your child respond)

Parent: Trace the triangle in the air and point to each number.

           (Pause, let your child respond)

Parent: As you're pointing, say what the number is and what you are going to do with it.

Child: 7 times 8 is 56; or 8 times 7 is 56; or 56 divided by 7 is 8; or 56 divided by 8 is 7.

(Once your child consistently points to the correct numbers, then quiz her.)

Parent: Close your eyes and look at your picture. What is 7 times 8?

Child: 56.

Parent: What is 8 times 7?

Child: I don't know. We haven't started our 8 facts yet.

Parent: Oh, that's ok. Just check your picture.

Child: 56?

Parent: Yes, that's very good. You just learned a new math fact. Now what is 56 divided by 8?

Child: I don't know how to do division.

Parent: That's OK. Just take a look at your picture. What do you see? A 56? The division sign? The number 8? Just follow your picture path. Where does it lead to?

Child: 7.

Parent: You're a genius! You just learned a division fact and started on your 8's!

Once this math fact family is learned well, then proceed to the next card with a different math facts family. If your child has difficulty remembering one of the numbers, then have her take a different color marker, or glitter, or something fun to highlight the number she misses.

This strategy needs to be repeated for at least *three consecutive days*.

Day 1: Encourage your child to just go through the process and notice what she knows.

Day 2: Review the triangle from yesterday and write out the completed facts.

Day 3: Have her review the facts and write them out again. By now, all facts should be "old friends."

That was multiplication and division. The same process can be used with addition and subtraction. Let me show you what this might look like, without going through the full dialogue of parent-child above. You can easily substitute in the plus and minus signs and the numbers.

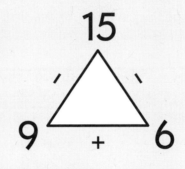

Math and Music Go Hand in Hand

If you're not a musician, be it vocalist or instrumental, you may not realize that musicians use math everyday. Look at the similarities between math and music.

Math	Music
Fractions ($\frac{1}{2}$, $\frac{1}{4}$, $\frac{1}{8}$)	Notes (half, quarter, eighth...) & Rhythm
Sets & Concepts	Keys (F, D....), Scales, Chords
Relationships between ratios, fractions, decimals	Frequency & Intervals (Harmonics, Tuning)

Few realize how closely connected math and music are. Math concepts can be enhanced through rhythm, sequencing, movement and sound experiences. The metronome is a mechanical device which can be set to beat a rhythm at any tempo. It can be used to teach sequencing and rhythm, both of which are important for math and reading fluency.

Music has a rhythm, as does all areas of learning, including reading and writing. And math, math has a rhythm as well.

And don't forget:
Remind your child to breathe. It's part of the solution to anything that puts pressure on him or makes him feel anxious, be it math, spelling, writing or reading.

It's unfortunate how some kids are evaluated by timed written tests. They may have beautiful learning strategies, yet crack under the pressure. What can you do to help your child prepare for any test without the added burden of increased stress anxiety? The next chapter gives you strategies to cover just that.

14

School Stressors—
Homework and Tests

I Hate Homework!

Child: I don't want to do my homework!

Parent: You spend more time complaining about your homework than doing it!

Child: This will take all night. I'm not going to do it!

Parent: You're just lazy!

Bad scene. Sound familiar? How miserable are you and your child, fighting everyday about homework? Do you feel that you are back in school, sitting daily with him to finish his homework? Some kids come right home and do their homework, or even finish it before they leave school. Others procrastinate, avoid, and then cram at the last minute, grumbling that there's too much and it's not fair.

Think about your daily schedule; you wake up early, make breakfast, throw in a load of wash, get the kids ready for school, run carpool duty, go to work, pick up the kids, take them to sports, bring them home, make dinner, start a load of wash, throw the wash in the dryer, help your kids do homework, get them ready for bed, read them a story and then lights out. When is there time for you? Ever feel trapped and overwhelmed? I would, and did.

Have you thought about your child also being overwhelmed? With all his extra-curricular activities and busy schedule, coming home to homework may create a similar feeling. Try this Activity to help him reduce the clutter and overwhelm in his mind.

Activity

Get Rid of the Clutter

Purpose: Organize and prioritize tasks.

Instructions to child:

Parent: Sit comfortably, eyes open or closed. Take a couple of big breaths.
(Pause)
Imagine yourself doing your homework. What do you notice?

Child: I'm sitting there surrounded by homework everywhere. Math, spelling, science—so much stuff, it's awful. It makes my head hurt.

Parent: Wow, it sounds like a mess. Take a few slow breaths, in and out.
(Pause)

Parent: What would you like to do with this mess?

Child: Get rid of some of it.

Parent: How can you get rid of the stuff?

Child: I'll put it in trash bags. Math in this one, spelling in that one, reading here …

Parent: Great, how about numbering the bags. That way you can take the bags that are most important and put the other bags away. How does that sound?

Child: OK.

(Give time for him to imagine doing that.)

Parent: Let's start with the "bag" that should be number one. Now, continue on with working the next "bag," number two. And continue on until all the mess is cleaned up.

Child: I'm done.

Parent: Very good. How do you feel now?

Child: Not so crazy!

Parent: Nice. Gently open your eyes. Now it's time to start your homework. Start with "bag number one." (Then continue through each subject).

Structuring on tasks with a "to do" list helps give closure and organization. This helps clear the clutter in the mind. Some people even number their "to do" list items. This puts things in perspective. Sometimes just by getting started with one of the homework items that "isn't so bad" puts your child in a working frame of mind that lets him get on a roll, and onto the next activity. Visualizing what you can complete helps displace the idea that there's so much you'll never get done.

Clutter Trick

When I have too much happening in my life, I feel pulled in so many directions that I don't even know where to start: go to work, pick up the cleaning, meet my kids for lunch, start dinner, clean the house ... and the list goes on. I'll bet you've had days like that.

I visualize myself putting "picture frames" around each task. Sometimes the task is so overwhelming that it starts breaking through the "frame". Then I make it a thicker frame, in my mind, to contain the task.

Next, I reduce the size of each frame by "squishing it down" with my hands. The less important tasks, like housecleaning for me, I make the frame very, very small; so small I can hardly see it. I take that little frame and toss it out the window. Whew! No need to worry about that task. One thing off my plate.

I visualize putting the least important task further away in my mind. I know that it will be there when I need to find it, but at least it's not cluttering my mind. After all, the dust will be here tomorrow. I decide on the most important task and move it front and center in my mind. If I get distracted, I squish down the "frames" and move them further away in my mind. These less important tasks become smaller concerns and don't clutter my mind anymore. That way, I can concentrate on my main priority. And get it done.

How to Complete Homework

What can you do if homework completion becomes a major concern? Start by talking to your child's teacher and see if there is anything else going on in school. How much time is his teacher expecting for homework? Is it reasonable for his age? If it is taking too much time? Is he wasting time doing other "stuff" or distracted? Is it too difficult? Or, is he really just complaining too much?

Talk to the parents of one or several of your child's classmates. If children who want to succeed all have the same complaint about the volume of work, that's quite different than your child being one of the few who's unable to handle the work volume. If the teacher thinks most children are keeping up on their own, but is adjusting expectations based on performance of children whose parents are doing the bulk of the work for them, then it isn't a level playing field anymore.

It might surprise you to know that some teachers can't visualize a parent working as hard as you do behind the scenes to help your child; you need to have the conversation that your child isn't lazy and really is trying to get work done. Perhaps your teacher is willing once a week to help prioritize homework assignments with your child. The main point here is that just by letting the teacher know how much you're working with your child; she might adjust expectations more realistically, or at least provide encouragement to your child.

Sure Ways to Complete Homework

- Establish a time and place for homework.
- Together, create a working space, free of distractions.
- Turn off the TV.
- Make an organizational chart. Commitment for follow-through for you and your child is important. Review Chapter 5, *Do It!*, for organizational chart templates. Rewards based on chart results are often helpful.
- Remember, it's *his* homework, not yours.
- His job is to do the work and face the consequences if he fails to do what's expected. You need to determine ahead of time what the consequences will be if he doesn't do the work. Don't spring a surprise.

Dr. H's INSIGHT

Time Tests

Many kids get nervous with tests, especially timed tests. The stress created often is based in fear: failing the test, receiving a bad grade, or concern that his parents will be mad if he doesn't do well. Stress can often shut down thinking and processing skills.

Have you ever been so nervous for a test that you can hardly see the writing on the paper? These problems start appearing at very young ages and continue throughout adult lives. Wouldn't it be ideal to have a strategy to prepare for testing situations?

Focusing on breathing makes a tremendous difference in being able to perform. Learning takes place most effectively when you child is relaxed and enjoying his work. What can you do to help him prepare for tests or stressful situations? You already know it—implement the *See It. Say It. Do It! Model* for test preparation!

When you introduce and practice these activities, be sure at the outset to pick a time and a place when and where you won't be interrupted. Turn your cell phone off, and let other family members know that you're having some quality time with your child. The same holds true for your child. You both have to believe that at this time there is nothing more important going on that's going to compete for your attention. By investing this time now, you're going to save a lot of time in the future.

Activity
The Clock Is Ticking!

Purpose: Discover a strategy for taking timed tests.

Instructions to child:

Parent: Sit comfortably with your eyes open or closed. Take a few breaths.
(Pause)
Imagine that you are getting ready for the CSAPs (standardized testing). Remember, all the test sections are timed.
What do you notice?

Child: All I see is a huge clock—tick, tick, tick.

Parent: Tell me more about the clock. Are you even in your picture?

Child: Nope. Just this huge clock that makes a loud noise. TICK, TICK, TICK!

(Carefully observe your child. Watch for signs of stress, tension, anxiety: breathing becoming shallow, sweating, or nervousness.)

Parent: How do you feel?

Child: I'm scared that I'll mess up the test and won't finish in time. I must be stupid!

Parent: Wow, that really worries you, huh?

Child: You know that I don't do good on timed tests. I can't even think, I get so scared.

Parent: I get it. That must really be scary for you (acknowledgment of feelings).
Let's stop for a second and take a breath. Breathe in and out. Breathe all the way into your tummy. Put your hand on your tummy and just breathe into your hand.
(Pause)
Do you still see that big clock?

Child: Uh-huh.

Parent: Anything else?

continued on next page

Child: No (showing signs of anxiety and nervousness).

Parent: (Observe him). How do you feel? Are you hot or cold?

Child: Really hot.

Parent: How hot?

Child: Like I'm burning up!

Parent: What would you like to do? Turn on a fan? Open a window? Jump in a swimming pool to cool off?

Child: How about opening a window?

Parent: OK. Imagine that you are opening a window to let the fresh cool air in. Let the air cool you down. Let it go through your entire body. What do you notice?

Child: (Big sigh from the child.) Phew … I just opened the window and some wind is blowing.

Parent: How does that make you feel?

Child: Better, not so hot.

Parent: So what do you notice now? What does the clock look like?

Child: Hey, the clock is gone!

Parent: Where did it go?

Child: I don't know.

Parent: What do you see in your picture now?

Child: I'm just sitting at my desk.

Parent: What are you doing?

Child: Playing with my pencils.

Parent: Tell me more about how you look.

Child: I'm very little, and looking scared. I'm holding my pencils very tight. (Observe your child. You might actually see his hands gripping tightly.)

Parent: How about shaking out your hands. Let those pencils go and just shake all the tightness out of your hands. Wiggle your fingers. Just shake, shake, shake!

(Encourage him to really move his hands and fingers.)

Now what would you like to do?

Child: Jump around!

Parent: Do it!

(Encourage him to jump, move, laugh.)

Parent: You look like you're having fun!

OK. It's time to take your test. Are you ready?

Child: I don't really want to take it, but I can. At least I'm not so hot and my fingers are wiggling. Hey, I seem to be bigger than I was before!

Parent: Nice! What else would you bring into your picture to help you on the test?

Child: All the answers!

Parent: Well, that would certainly be helpful. How can you do that?

Child: I can write all the stuff I learned on a sheet and save the sheet in my head.

Parent: And anytime you could check your answer sheet in your head for information? Is that right?

Child: Yeah!

Parent: So imagine how it feels now—going into your classroom, breathing with the window open, wiggling your hands and toes and having all the answers in your head **(See It!)**.

Child: I think I can take my test now.

Parent: Make yourself strong and smart. What can you say to remind you of feeling like this?

Child: I'm smart and have all the answers in my head **(Say It!)**.

Parent: You're the best! Now gently open you eyes and shake out all your wiggles. Practice everyday saying, "I am smart and have all the answers in my head." Say it while you see and feel yourself breathing with the window open and wiggling your arms and fingers.

This was great fun!

Ready to study for the test now?

Child: OK **(Do It!)**.

Be creative and bring in movement throughout the visualization process. When your child creates his own silly picture, there is a much better chance that the *See It. Say It. Do It! Model* process will be useful. Ultimately the plan is to sit down to take a test with the idea that you're prepared and expecting to pass, rather than being stressed and expecting to fail.

Tests come in all shapes and sizes. Some have greater importance than others. Below are additional strategies that may be effective for preparing for timed tests.

Release the Time Pressure

If your child complains that he has too much homework or that it takes too long, you need to do a quick assessment.

Ask her and her teacher how long the homework assignments should take. Does your child agree or not with your teachers estimate?

If she agrees, great. If not, ask her how much time she feels she needs. If you have a 20 minute assignment (per your teacher), but your child often needs additional time to complete the task, then ask her if 30 minutes (or whatever you decide upon) is enough.

Now, get a timer, preferably an old kitchen timer where you can turn the dial to the agreed upon time and watch it click down. Set the clock to 30 minutes, or whatever the agreed time is. The rule for this night's homework assignment is that she will only work for 30 minutes. When the timer goes off, whether or not the homework is completed, she is done with her homework (make sure you have worked this arrangement with her teacher). However, if she was messing around, losing attention and concentration, the timer is shut off until she is back on task. Then the timer is re-started.

Most of the time, she will finish her assignments way ahead of the proposed time. Having an "end point," which is represented by the clock, is similar to having a frame or box around the task, as used in the "Get Rid of the Clutter" Activity. This represents closure and organization for her. Now she sees that it is possible to complete the task.

The "Clock is Ticking" Activity teaches her how to start working under time pressure, her own time pressure. It also builds awareness as to how much time she wastes when she sees you shut off the timer when she messes around!

There are a few rules you might consider creating. Discuss these rules ahead of time, so that your child knows in advance what to expect. Be consistent with the rules. For example, all homework has to be finished before the TV or computer games are turned on. Kids really buckle down when there is an important show on TV. It's amazing how fast they complete their homework.

Preparing for the Big One

The *See It. Say It. Do It! Model* strategies for test preparation work for older kids as well. And they can be adapted for adults! It certainly worked well for my daughter when she faced a major test.

It was National Board time. My daughter, Becky, was preparing for her National Board Certification Test. She knew the material, but was still very worried and dreading testing day. She asked if I'd help her prepare for the test. Here is how we worked together:

Mom: Becky, sit comfortably, eyes open or closed. Now take a few
    breaths in and out, in and out.

(Pause)

Great. Now, let your imagination take you to a place where you feel
    safe. A place where you are very relaxed. A place where you
    can really be who you are. Where would that be?

Becky: My yoga studio.

Mom: Nice. Describe how you feel and what you notice in your
    yoga studio.

Becky: I'm in my favorite yoga outfit, orange top with black yoga pants.
    I'm sitting on my purple mat; breathing in calmly and letting go of
    tension. It's very peaceful.

Mom: Imagine moving into one of your yoga postures; an easy posture which you can move in and out of very smoothly. Just notice how that feels.

Becky: Good.

Mom: Now, move into a more difficult posture; one that really challenges you. What happens?

Becky: I start getting a lot of thoughts in my head. My first thought is that it's too hard. I just want to quit. But my teacher keeps telling me to breathe and relax into the posture. Eventually I relax and go as far as I can go into the posture. Then I let it go and move to the next posture.

Mom: That's great. What if you imagined that every question on your Certification Test was a yoga posture? You treat every question just like a separate posture. You breathe, relax and go as far as you can go. Imagine sitting in the room taking your test, one question at a time. Move smoothly through the easy ones. Just breathe and relax into the harder ones and do the best you can. Then let it go and move on to the next question. Try it.

Becky: That's pretty interesting. I don't freak out about each question that way. Hey, I could make my Test like going to a yoga class. What do you think?

Mom: What a super idea. Just as you practice your yoga daily, you could practice your Test preparation daily as well, knowing that when you relax into each posture (question), you have full access to think clearly and efficiently.

Becky embraced this strategy. She showed up on test day wearing her favorite yoga outfit. She sat down and started with a few breaths before looking at the Test. Then she addressed each question just as would do each yoga posture. Becky passed her Test with flying colors. She was excited that her preparation reduced her anxiety and stress, allowing her to think more clearly.

This yoga example may not work with your child as well as it worked with Becky. Why? Becky is passionate about yoga. That is her special place. That may not be your child's special place.

The key is to help your child find a place where he is relaxed, calm, happy, and thinks easily. This is where he's most likely able to succeed. His place may be in the mountains snowboarding, in the swimming pool or his room. It's his choice where he goes.

The Activities in this chapter addressed homework and test preparation. Where else might you use these Activities? What about competition in sports or music? The fears and anxieties are often similar. The strategy is also similar. The content of the script can be modified to be specific for the competition. Read on to the next chapter to see how this works.

15

Improving Performance in Sports and Music

"**D**o you believe in miracles?" shouted broadcaster Al Michaels as he completed the final countdown at the dramatic win during the men's hockey medal-round at the 1980 Olympic Winter Games. It was an unbelievable upset. Team USA, made up of collegiate players who practiced together for a year and a half, beat the very experienced Soviet Union Team, considered the best hockey team in the world. Eventually, Team USA went on to the Final medal-round and beat Finland to win the Gold Medal.

So how did this miracle happen? Team USA Coach, Herb Brooks, held numerous tryout camps, which included psychological testing, before selecting a roster from hundreds of prospects. He scheduled four months of exhibition games across Europe and North America. The Team was no match for the European Skill, so Brooks emphasized speed, conditioning and discipline. "He messed with our minds at every opportunity," said Mike Ramsey one of the players.

Brooks worked to unite the team. His tactical moves were brilliant. In the end, the underdogs won. The impossible dream came true. "It may just be the single most indelible moment in all of U.S. sports history," wrote *Sports Illustrated* of Team USA's improbable gold medal run at the 1980 Winter Olympics. "One that sent an entire nation into a frenzy."

Brooks passed away in 2003. At his funeral, Rev. John Malone of Assumption Catholic Church in St. Paul, Minnesota, said:

> Most miracles are dreams made manifest. Herbie had a dream. The players had a dream. If we could all dream ... and do our best, we could make this a better world. It's within our reach.[1]

What a great inspirational story. I remember the tension and excitement watching the games; tears in our eyes when Jim Craig, the goalie, skated around the ice with the United States flagged draped over him. What a moment for the Team, and for millions of people watching and believing in them. Even today, I get chills just thinking about it. That shows how powerful and lasting visualization can be, not just for competitors, but for spectators!

The Extra Edge

Nike's famous swoosh logo is accompanied by the line, "Just Do It!" But there's a lot of "Just See It" and "Just Say It" necessary before being able to Just Do It! Numerous stories and examples are presented throughout *See It. Say It. Do It!* on the importance of visualization with athletes. Coaches and athletes know what separates the mediocre athletes from the champions, where hundredths of seconds or tenths of an inch count. Numerous athletes are turning to visualization training to take their game to the next level. When practiced, there is improvement in consistency and accuracy of the skill.

The most successful athletes visualize (**See It!**) before their pitch, jump, swing, run, shoot or swing. Just as positive visualization helps to create top performance, negative visualization will often impair performance. It's the expectation to succeed, versus the expectation to fail, as discussed in the previous chapter about test anxiety. Think about the kid who gets ready to serve the volleyball, thinking, "I'm going to hit the ball into the net. Just watch." And what do you think happens? He hits it into the net! Or what about the young gymnast who keeps imagining she'll fall off the bars? She does. What we bring our attention to usually happens.

Visualization training may be focused in different areas:

- Mental practice of specific skills

- Improve confidence

- Problem solving

- Reduce stress and anxiety

- Preparation for performance

- Maintain mental readiness even during injury recovery time

What Happened to Our LPGA Golfer?

Remember the golfer in Chapter 2, *Your Child's Vision Development?* Her first first years on the Ladies Professional Golf Association Tour were a struggle. She had eye coordination problems and was losing confidence in her game. Would you like to know the rest of the story?

She received vision therapy for her eye coordination problems. She was a very motivated patient—time and money were key factors. She took time off the Tour, missing multiple financial opportunities during her therapy. This LPGA golfer did exceptionally well in vision therapy and eliminated her eye coordination problem within a few months.

I couldn't write a better script for what happened. After completing her vision therapy, she enjoyed a successful career as a six-time winner and is ranked among the top in all-time career earnings on the LPGA. She is still an advocate for vision therapy. As she said regarding visualization or the mind's eye:

> When you can't center your eyes, you can't quiet your mind,
> and you need that quiet for your concentration—that's when
> the third eye (or the ability to visualize) comes into play.

There is a bonus to this story. We found out later that her reading had also improved significantly. Professional golfers spend countless hours on the road, travelling from tournament to tournament. My golfer wished she could read more, to occupy her travel time on the Tour. She couldn't. Reading for her was such hard work, so fatiguing, that she hated it. After her vision therapy, she became a much more comfortable and avid reader.

When Do I Practice?

There is no right or wrong way to practice visualizing. It can be done on or off the field; individually or in a group. It could be a long imagery where the entire team visualizes their plays in the locker room before the start of each practice. Or a very short one (a few seconds or minutes), where a high jumper practices seeing himself run towards the bar, knowing exactly where his take-off spot is, and then seeing himself float over the bar and gently land on the mat.

My daughters, both competitive gymnasts from nine to fourteen years of age, found that bedtime was a great time to visualize their routines. Remember the balloon trip visualization in Chapter 1, *What is Visualization?* That's exactly what we did. Before bedtime, we lay on the bed, closed our eyes and took a balloon trip together, using the script for the Activity. We started with breathing and relaxation. Then it was time to get out of the balloon, once we reached the clouds. Here is a sample of what happened in the clouds with my youngest, Becky:

Mom: Let's park our balloon. Climb out of the basket and find a cloud where you want to go through your gymnastic routines. Make sure this cloud is strong, supportive and safe. When you fine your cloud, let me know.

Becky: OK, here's a big, fluffy one.

Mom: Super! Which event do you want to start on?

Becky: Floor.

Mom: What is your goal for floor?

Becky: To hit all of my elements (flips, twists, dance moves).

Mom: Say something about how good you are as a gymnast.

Becky: I am strong and have great balance!

Mom: OK. Turn on your music. As soon as it starts, go through your routine. Remember, the clouds are there to support you.

I could not only see Becky visualizing her routine, I could feel her muscles twitch and jerk as she would do her flips and twists in her mind. When she completed this routine, she would throw her hands up high, saluting the judges and the crowd that she is finished, just as she does in competition.

Mom: Take a rest for a few seconds. When you're ready, which event is next?

Becky: The beam.

Mom: OK. What's your goal?

Becky: To stay on the beam!

Teach your child to make her goal using positive words, rather than negative like, "Not to fall off the beam." Saying a phrase like "fall off" can influence and bring attention to the mind to "fall off!"

Becky would sometimes fall off the beam, and was developing a fear of performing back handsprings on the beam. When she reported that she was scared of the next move, I said:

Mom: Becky, do you feel safe or is there anything else you need to protect you on beam? Remember, those clouds are just for you, to support you and to keep you safe. Sometimes she asked for a safety rope tied to her, and sometimes the clouds were enough to give her the confidence to perform the elements.

Once Becky completed her four routines, then we would go through the medal ceremony. Seeing herself on the podium receiving her medal, Becky's smile said it all. Then it was time to turn off the lights and go to sleep.

This routine lasted for years, even when I was out of town. Becky would call me at my hotel and ask to be taken on a balloon trip, to get ready for her next meet.

Start It Now!

As Jack Nicklaus, one of the greatest golfers, once said:

> I never hit a shot, not even in practice, without having a very
> sharp, in-focus picture of it in my head. It's like a color movie.

If famous golfers like Jack Nicklaus and other athletes can visualize and succeed, so can your child!

Practicing with your child at an early age gives her a lifetime skill. As you can see in the practice with Becky, she didn't just picture the routine in her mind, she felt and moved physically. The pictures in her mind created motor responses; teaching her muscles to do exactly what she wants them to do. The brain can't tell the difference between whether you are actually performing or imagining you are performing.

The combination of solid physical training and confidence really comes together in sports. Allison Arnold, Ph.D., is founder of Head Games and a consultant to USA Gymnastics, U.S. Figure Skating, amateur, professional and collegiate athletes. She says:

> It's never too early to teach your child the basics of mental
> training. Training the mind is no different from training
> the body.[2]

This type of training used to be reserved for the Olympic or star athletes. It's now common for more kids to learn about the interconnection between the mind and the body. Savvy coaches implement it as part of their basic training when they start working with teams and individuals.

If your child has not utilized visualization for practice, she might need a little experience to see the connection between her mind and her sports performance. Try this:

Activity

Sports Preparation Visualization for Younger Kids

Purpose: Demonstrate how a little imagination can help their performance.

Instructions to child:
Parent: Stand with your feet together and jump with both feet as far as you can. Let's see how far you can go.

(Child jumps. Mark the spot where she lands.)

Parent: Now let's do it again. But first imagine that you can jump farther. (Pause. Let her picture the mark you made where she landed, then see herself landing past it, and then you drawing the new mark).

Parent: Now try it again.

(Child jumps further.)

Parent: It's like magic! Isn't that cool how your imagination can help you?

Parent: Each time you have a new game or goal, remember how you can use your imagination to help.

Try another activity, and remind her to use her imagination to help her. Keep building on her success until she understands how it works and becomes part of her routine.

The next Activity can be used for any sport. Modify it specifically for your child's sport by filling in the blanks.

Activity

Sports Preparation Visualization for Older Kids

Purpose: Learn how to apply visualization to sports practice.

Instructions to child:

Parent: Find a relaxing place to sit or lie down.

Breathe in and out (pause). In and out.

Gently close your eyes and allow your body to relax.

Now, when you are ready, see yourself getting ready to play (whatever his sport is).

Let's start by getting dressed.

Put on your ___ (guide him through his specific clothing, uniform, equipment).

How do you feel?

Child: ___ (response)

Parent: Go to ___ (the gym, field, school—or wherever the athletic event will be).

Imagine yourself looking strong, confident and ready to play.

Take a look at the ___ (field, court, etc.).

How does it look?

Child: ___ (response)

Parent: What is the weather like?

Child: ___ (response)

Parent: Who else is there?

Child: ___ (response)

Parent: How do you feel?

Child: ___ (response)

Parent: Are you nervous?

Child: Yes.

(Observe your child's response.)

Parent: Where do you feel nervous?

Child: In my tummy.

Parent: Oh, that's very common. Just pay attention to your tummy. Try putting your hand on your tummy and breathe into your hand. Does that help?

Child: No.

Parent: That's OK. You can take anything you'd like with you in your visualization. Is there something you would like to bring with you to help you?

continued on next page

Child: Yeah, how about my favorite Transformer.

Parent: Good idea—take your favorite Transformer with you. Now how to you feel?

Child: Better.

Parent: Remember, your pictures in your mind are yours! You can always imagine anything to help yourself. Do you know that?

Child: Uh-huh.

Parent: Are you feeling ready to play now?

Child: Yep!

Parent: OK! Imagine yourself _____ (go through the routine of the sport, step by step).

Say something positive about yourself. (See sample declaration list.)

Game's over. Proudly walk off the field (or court) and "pat" yourself on the back for doing your best. Now shake hands (congratulate) with your teammates (and/or opponents).

See yourself receiving your rewards trophies, or recognition (whatever is appropriate for the activity).

Declarations for Sports

See It. Say It. Do It! Model is woven throughout sports. Chapter 4, *Say It!* emphasizes the importance of declarations and management of your child's thoughts. This is a critical element of sports preparation.

Team USA's Coach Herb Brooks was a master at declarations. The night of the big win, he told his team, "Nine out of ten times we'd play this team and they would beat us. But not tonight ... because tonight is our night. Tonight we win!" That's called a declaration **(Say It!).**

How about helping your child when he struggles at the free throw line in basketball? How successful do you think your child will be at making a free throw when he keeps getting a message from his mind, "You're going to miss it." He has the ability to learn how to manage his thoughts and pictures in his mind; to have the skill to calm his mind, change his images to positive pictures, make a declaration like, "I can do it!," and then shoot the free throw (**Do It!**).

Here is a sample of declarations related to sports which are helpful to counter negative thoughts.

Negative Thoughts	*Inspired Declarations*
I'm a loser.	I'm a winner.
I don't deserve to be here.	I belong here.
I'm a klutz.	I'm smooth and powerful.
I choke and mess up.	I take risks and play my best.
What if I blow it?	It's OK to make mistakes—I learn from them.
I don't want to let my coach or parents down.	My coach believes in me; I believe in myself.
I'm stupid.	I am proud of myself.

Having your child say nice things to himself is not bragging. It is building a sense of self-worth and confidence. Acknowledgment of himself and his abilities is important in growing not only as an athlete, but as a person. As the great American boxer and three-time World Heavyweight Champion, Muhammad Ali, once said:

> In order to be a great champion, you must believe that you are the best ... and if you're not, pretend that you are.

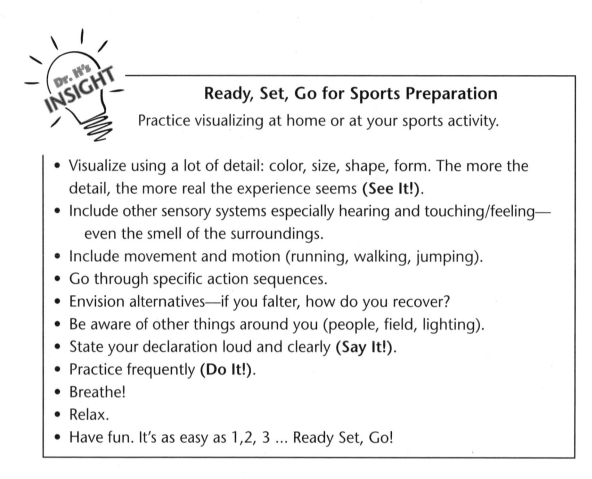

Ready, Set, Go for Sports Preparation

Practice visualizing at home or at your sports activity.

- Visualize using a lot of detail: color, size, shape, form. The more the detail, the more real the experience seems **(See It!)**.
- Include other sensory systems especially hearing and touching/feeling— even the smell of the surroundings.
- Include movement and motion (running, walking, jumping).
- Go through specific action sequences.
- Envision alternatives—if you falter, how do you recover?
- Be aware of other things around you (people, field, lighting).
- State your declaration loud and clearly **(Say It!)**.
- Practice frequently **(Do It!)**.
- Breathe!
- Relax.
- Have fun. It's as easy as 1,2, 3 ... Ready Set, Go!

Have your child practice her visualization every day. She shouldn't wait until the day of the performance, when she is apt to be stressed and nervous. This activity needs to be integrated and automatic for it to be useful during stressful times.

Sports preparation starts with each child working on her own personal preparation. If your child plays on a team, then the next step is for your child to bring herself as strong, powerful and confident as possible to her team. The next activity is an example of what you or the coach might say to your team.

Activity

Sports Preparation Visualization for a Team

Purpose: Learn how to apply visualization to team sports practice.

Instructions to team:

Coach or *Parent:* Think of a time when you and the team played a big match; when you were all working well together and everyone was on their game. Each played with power and focus, yet relaxed. Imagine seeing and hearing your teammates. You are all super athletes playing together as one; sharing with each other; supporting each other and sharing the highs and the lows together. You help each other improve; knowing each other's strengths and weakness. You know you belong here, being part of a larger whole unit. Think of your team goals. Believe in each other. Have fun. Be proud of your team and your hard work together, trusting each other.

Now, think of a word that reminds you of these feelings, pictures, sounds of teamwork and top performance you've just imagined. Say this word over and over again to bring you back to this team experience. Write *your word* on a paper and plaster copies of it all over your room.

Say *your word* every day, at home and before practice. Know why you are here; to have fun, learn, and work together. Ready? Break!

I Hate Sports! Now What?

Not all kids like sports. Don't be surprised or concerned. I strongly support that all kids should participate in some type of *exercise program* for their physical fitness and health, whether it be a group sport like football, baseball, basketball, hockey, or soccer or an individual one, like walking, running, dance, gymnastics, swimming, or martial arts. It can be just for fun or more for competition.

Allowing your child to find his passion is key. Maybe he is interested in the arts or music. Being a musician myself, I did not participate in structured sports activities as a kid. I loved to ride my bike, played tennis and racketball. My passion was in music. The challenges of being part of an orchestra and a musical theater group are very similar as those in sports; the tryouts, competition, performances, making the group. Any group activity requires harmony and chemistry between individuals to produce something greater than the sum of its parts.

Come Sing with Us … and Visualize the Medal

The visualizations and scripts in this chapter can easily be adapted to prepare for a musical event or art project. Amy discovered that when she joined the Sweet Adelines International Singers, a world-renowned chorus with members of all ages. Amy shared,

Our International chorus has been competing for at least 20 years. We constantly strive to find coaches and musical leadership to help us in our journey to win that gold medal. We bring in and hire mostly vocal coaches and then also work with performance coaches that help us with characterization and movement. We had been doing fine with all of those coaches, but still somehow we still could not score better than 6th, usually placing between 11th and 20th. Hundreds of choruses compete to qualify for the International Competition.

Our director and our management team came up with a new concept to move us into the next level. Basically it was this: if we couldn't **internally visualize** ourselves winning a gold medal, then it most likely would not happen.

We needed to find a way to convince ourselves that we were worthy of a gold medal and that we could see ourselves as a champion level chorus.

Our Chorus hired what we called a "Mental Coach." She worked with our Chorus beginning in 2003. First she had to get to know us—we were different from her previous clients. She had previously worked with professional athletes, so a 165 women barbershop chorus was a whole new concept for her.

She first worked with us on what our goals were—where we had been and where we wanted to go. How did we picture (visualize) ourselves currently? What did we think the future Chorus look like? Once that was said, we laid out our plans on how we were going to get there.

How did that new "image" change what we were currently doing and what new things were we going to have to do, and change, in order to reach our new goals?

We put together action plans and she worked with our "mental state" so that we could get to that next level. One of the problems with a big group like ours, unlike individual visualizations, is that we have to trust one another that we are doing the homework (vocally, mentally and physically). Not only that, but during a performance we have to be completely "present to what we are doing" and not be distracted by the audience responses or internal mistakes. Either can throw off your own individual performance, which in turn can throw off the person next to you. It is quite a balance of trust and confidence.

Our first year working with her was 2003. The next year, we placed 4th, our best result. We continued our work with her and placed 2nd in 2006, and since then, have placed in the top five. We know that we are on the right road; we just have to keep working hard.

We are a non-profit organization and unfortunately we are unable to continue to pay for her expertise. However, she taught us some invaluable lessons and we have truly opened our eyes to see and believe that we can and will win that gold medal someday soon. Thanks to our visualizations, we know that we can.

I experienced the same types of lessons in music that an athlete experiences in sports. What are some of those lessons? Let's review.

Lessons of Life

Sports, music and other activities are training grounds for life. The lessons your child learns, beyond the skill of the activity, are endless: teamwork, leadership, commitment, physical strength, motivation, preparation, mental toughness, and confidence. Your child may not always experience a **Ta-Dah!** like Team USA Hockey and the rest of the nation did. But with continued practice, learning, and support, he is creating and growing into a powerful person. As a parent, I would view that as a **Ta-Dah!**

> There are two things you as a parent can give your child; one is roots and the other is wings. (Unknown author.)

Dr. H's INSIGHT

The *See It. Say It. Do It! Model* is designed to give you strategies for both—creating roots and wings for your child. His confidence is essential for preparing him to develop his wings for freedom, independence and success. Even the best of athletes and musicians experience confidence erosion at times. The next chapter gives you tools to help build your child's confidence.

Part Four

Personal Growth

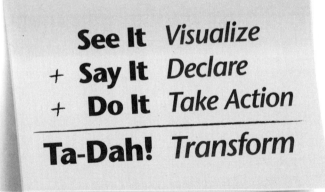

16

Building Self-Confidence

It is painful watching your child struggle with lack of confidence and self-doubt. The comments like, "I'm not good enough," "I'm stupid," "Nobody likes me," are destructive.

You can't give your child self-confidence. As much as you frequently say positive things to him, it often backfires. Your child needs to see and feel the confidence for himself. Children must learn to trust themselves. When your child is confident, he trusts his own judgment and abilities. He is courageous to take risks in new situations, knowing that he has strategies to help him learn and be reliable. He builds confidence step-by-step with each experience.

Here are a few stories of how one teacher impacted many of her students by teaching them about taking responsibility, pride and acknowledgment.

Kindergarteners Say Great Things

Barry had learning problems and struggled in kindergarten. He completed an assignment, but didn't think he did a very good job. His teacher, whose name was Pat, smiled and told him to "Be proud of what you did, as long as you tried your best." She also told him about the "Pat Technique," created by her. The *Pat Technique* simply is "patting yourself on the back" when you have done something that you are proud of. Some kids (and adults) have a very difficult time accepting acknowledgment. It starts with your child's own pat on his back.

The next day, Barry worked diligently on his assignment. He completed it and told his teacher that he did his best. He asked her, "Is it OK if I *pat* myself on my back?" His teacher smiled and said, "Of course! You deserve it. You did your best."

Susie was making a "book" for her dad to give him when he came back from his trip. It was getting late and her mother asked her to finish her project and put her stuff away. Susie said, "No, I need to take pride in what I'm doing and be proud of my work. I haven't finished my book for Dad yet!" Susie's mother was quite surprised by her response and allowed her to finish her project. Susie had just learned in class about having pride and being proud. She was practicing what she learned.

Greg was lying on the floor with all his other kindergarten classmates. His teacher read them a story, and then asked them to draw a picture about the story. Greg didn't want to share his picture because his picture didn't look like his classmates. He said he didn't see a picture of the story in his mind. The next day his teacher discussed the fact that each student's drawing will be different, and everyone's drawing was important. People just see and understand different things. It's not about being right or wrong. Being different was OK.

After story time the next day, Greg was excited to share his picture with his class, knowing it was OK to be different. His teacher emphasized to the class that they need to understand that it doesn't have to look a certain way. That's the beauty of drawing—it teaches kids to express themselves visually, see the differences, share the stories, and build confidence in their skills. What Greg needed, and got, was a safe, nurturing, non-critical environment.

Mommy, the Goblins Are Back!

When my daughter, Annie, was three-years-old, she often woke me in the middle of the night because of bad dreams. "There are goblins in my bed, with big noses poking me," she would cry. I would hold her and comfort her, but she had difficulty calming down. I would ask her to describe what the goblins looked like. With big tears in her eyes, she said, "They are big, ugly and very scary."

I asked her what she would like to do with those scary goblins. "I want to jump on them and squish them down so they were little teeny funny things; and pinch their noses ..." Annie added that she wanted to tickle them until they would "laugh."

So she pretended and jumped on them (in bed) and tickled them until all of us were laughing. The sillier she made them, the less scared she was. Eventually our silliness created such a non-threatening picture in her mind that she became friendly with those goblins and they no longer bothered her.

Note that I did not say things to her like, "Oh, don't be scared of those goblins. They are just make-believe." I acknowledged her fear. Remember, the brain can't tell the difference between real experiences and visualized experiences. Those goblins look and seem very real to a three-year-old.

I also didn't say, "Oh, you're all right, I'll protect you." I wanted to find a way to empower her, even at the age of three, to learn how to change the pictures in her mind and not just rely on external forces to take care of personal fears.

Dealing with Bullies

One of the challenges kids face at school is that of bullying. There seems to always be at least one who relishes terrorizing others. Sometimes their victims are little and sometimes mentally or physically disadvantaged. What happens if your child is the target?

Deborah L. Sandella, Ph.D., R.N., and award-winning author of *Releasing the Inner Magician, Ways to Find a Peaceful and Happy Life* created the RIM™ Method, a cutting edge technique that allows you to:

> Navigate the "rim" between actual experience and imagination to stimulate rapid results and accelerated healing. Over the last few years, RIM has expanded my application of visualization personally and professionally. RIM acts on the neuro-sensory system to transform latent self-sabotaging images/beliefs/feelings into new heartfelt successful ones. Previous emotional triggers lose their charge, and you find yourself automatically behaving

in empowered ways—just like magic! You feel physically lighter, emotionally clearer and intuitively directed.[1]

Using the RIM Method, Dr. Sandella demonstrated how the visualization process can be effectively used to help Britt, one of my vision therapy patients, gain the confidence of safety and courage.

Britt was a sixth grader who has been diagnosed with learning disabilities, attention deficit disorder, and sensory processing disorder. She was academically and emotionally below her age level. She had recently been bullied by other children and did not want to go to school.

Due to the complexity and emotional involvement of this patient, the specific details of the session will not be included. Dr. Sandella worked with Britt for over an hour, using the RIM Method.

A summary of what she did with Britt was to have her imagine ways that she could feel safe and protected from the noise and roughness of the "annoying boys" in her class. It was important that Britt become aware of her senses; the colors, sounds, and feelings—just like you've learned from other Activities in *See It. Say It. Do It!* Britt imagined that she had a beautiful bubble of protection around her where she could hear her favorite music playing in the background and a special friend whispering encouragement and support in her ear.

Through use of the RIM process, Britt saw herself becoming larger and stronger. She now felt she had inner resources she could employ to protect her from the taunts and mean words of the other kids. At the end of the session, Britt visibly looked more confident. Months later, her mother reported to my staff that Britt was using her inner resources and effectively confronting aggressive behavior in her classes.

Children get bullied all too often. Most do not have learning problems like Britt, but they do exhibit lack of self-confidence which bullies take advantage of. As a parent, there are times when you need to reach out for professional help. If you have concerns about your child, start with the school. They may have a program that you can tap into, or you may need to get outside help from a psychologist, vision therapist or RIM facilitator like Britt did.

Get the Popcorn: It's Movie Time Again!

What can you do as a parent to help build your child's confidence? You can give him opportunities to succeed and acknowledge his success. You can coach him on strategies to be successful and overcoming the obstacles when he fails. Learning from failure is often the most valuable lesson, if your child is able to get beyond the upset he created from his mistake.

Do you remember in Chapter 3, *See It!* how powerful it was for your child to utilize all senses when building his visualization? This next Activity demonstrates how this strategy empowers your child and helps him find courage and confidence. The Confidence Movie can be used when there has been a situation where your child has been criticized or involved in conflict.

Activity

The Confidence Movie

Purpose: Building courage and confidence after criticism or conflict.

Instructions to child:

Parent: Sit comfortably with open or closed eyes.
　Imagine the situation where the kids made fun of you today. Tell me what's happening in the movie in your head?

Child: I was in gym class today and struck out in softball. All the kids booed me.

Parent: How did you feel?

Child: I really felt bad and wished I wasn't there.

Parent: How did you look?

Child: Awful! I was crying. All the kids were big and I was just a little nobody.

Parent: Gosh, what a hard thing for you. Let's try something, ok?
Pretend that you are sitting in a movie theater getting ready to watch your movie of what happened today in the softball game. You're watching the movie of yourself and the other kids.

Now start the movie in your mind all over again, but before you do, change the size of yourself, making yourself very big. If you want, you can also change the size of the other kids so that they are not bigger than you. Also, you can imagine and add anything in this movie to decrease the hurt you felt. Try adding silly music, like circus music. Or give all of the team funny uniforms. Remember, you are in charge of your pictures. You can imagine and create anything you want in your mind.

(Pause)

Play the movie again from beginning to end. Watch what happens when the kids are no longer bigger than you.
(Pause)

This time, play the movie again in your mind and put yourself in the movie as being strong and confident.
Now what happens?

Child: At least the kids aren't laughing at me anymore. They're cheering for me to get a hit. I still may strike out, but it's not so bad this time. I'll get a hit next time I'm up to bat.

This strategy can be used with kids of all ages. It's what I used with Annie when she had to "squish the goblins."

Children start building confidence at a very young age. They learn disappointment and failure early in their life, especially if criticized and judged.

Do's and Don'ts of Self-Confidence

Over the years, I've developed *Do's* and *Don'ts* for kids in building confidence ... for my own children as well as my patients. Here's my list for helping your child build self-confidence:

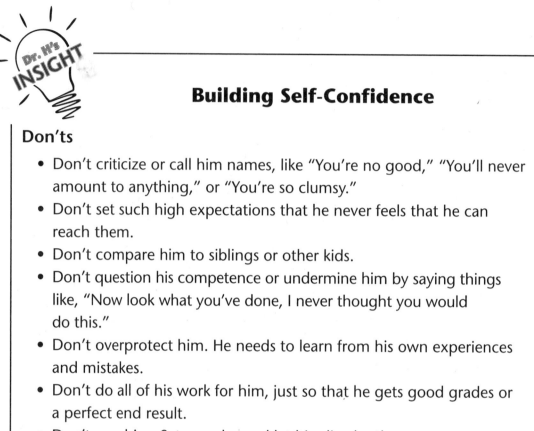

Building Self-Confidence

Don'ts

- Don't criticize or call him names, like "You're no good," "You'll never amount to anything," or "You're so clumsy."
- Don't set such high expectations that he never feels that he can reach them.
- Don't compare him to siblings or other kids.
- Don't question his competence or undermine him by saying things like, "Now look what you've done, I never thought you would do this."
- Don't overprotect him. He needs to learn from his own experiences and mistakes.
- Don't do all of his work for him, just so that he gets good grades or a perfect end result.
- Don't nag him. Set up rules and let him live by the consequences.
- Don't dwell on his weaknesses or what he falls short on.
- Don't be a "helicopter parent," hovering all the time. If your child did mediocre work, it's mediocre. Don't ask a teacher to raise a grade because he got something you didn't like or want.

Building Self-Confidence

Do's

- Create a safe, secure environment for your child.
- Make sure you make time to listen very carefully to your child.
- Help him find an extracurricular activity he likes, such as sports, music, or art. It needs to be *his* choice, not your wish for him, even if his choice bores you.
- Give him plenty of encouragement and support; be honest and kind.
- Reassure him that it is normal and okay to make mistakes, by saying things like, "I guess that didn't work for you this time. Next time maybe you can try doing it a different way."
- Model confident behavior. If he hears you tearing yourself down, remember, you are his model and he can easily copy that behavior.
- Provide and support him with tutoring or coaching if he struggles academically or in extra-curricular activities.
- Share your own personal stories of your struggles as a kid and what you did to overcome your obstacles.
- Believe in your child and let him know you love him.
- Accept any of your child's fears as being genuine, even if you think they are trivial.
- Laugh with your child, not at him.
- Use the *See It. Say It. Do It! Model* to provide strategies for him to create and take action. Positive declarations are important in decreasing negative self-talk.

Confidence Summing Up

The *See It. Say It. Do It! Model* provides you with strategies to help your child discover his own abilities and answers. It is designed to be very honoring and respectful of your child. It is not about the right or wrong way of doing things, it's about creating possibilities and finding ways to make them happen. The *See It. Say It. Do It! Model* was developed to create successful students and confident kids.

Let's come back to Harry Potter. In the *Sorcerer's Stone*, the reader first learns of the Invisibility Cloak, a magical cape that belonged to Harry's father. Harry could simply envelop himself, his friends, or anything he could get the cloak around, and no one could see it or them. They felt strong, secure and protected, just like Britt did in her pink bubble.

Your child can visualize that he or she is surrounded with safety, strength and courage. An Invisibility Cloak is not needed. Although you can't give your child self-confidence, you can share with him the gift of visualization. It will be as though you opened up the door to a beautiful foreign language on the path to personal growth. And, as Dr. Seuss wrote, "Oh the Places You'll Go!"

Dr. H's Final Insight …

"If you imagine it you can achieve it. If you dream it you can become it."

Those words of William Arthur Ward are the perfect way to bring *See It. Say It. Do It!* to a close. Your child's confidence proportionately increases with the success he feels at home and school. That success is rooted in his ability to learn how to look within and become aware of all the possibilities he can achieve.

He learns that he can take charge of his thoughts, visualizations, declarations and thereby takes action in all areas of his life. He becomes more confident and has strategies when he needs to overcome barriers and obstacles. And he becomes more successful in school and more interested in the joy of learning. It's the **Ta-Dah!**, "I did it!"

Parenting is an awesome and very challenging responsibility. This is your opportunity to explore and create possibilities for yourself. Take a few moments for yourself; relax, breathe and visualize yourself as a great parent. One who has the love, wisdom, strength, power and compassion to provide for your child. Teach your son or daughter to be a lifetime learner.

Know that you are the role model for your children. Take a risk yourself! Use *See It. Say It. Do It!* to guide you to guide your child. When you "Walk your talk," it's so much easier for your child to follow in your footsteps.

I wrote this book to exemplify how the power of the *See It. Say It. Do It! Model* can transform you personally. Little did I realize how the process of writing this book would transform me. I utilized the *See It. Say It. Do It! Model* throughout my writing journey; creating my visualization of the completed book (**See It!**), declaration of "I am a strong writer" (**Say It!**), and action plans to keep me on track (**Do It!**).

The issues I encountered in the process of writing this book; overcoming my frustrations of writing, the time deadlines, the overwhelming pressure of it—really put me to the test. It was amazing how stories and incidents occurred in my life, just at the appropriate time as I was writing a specific chapter. What kept me motivated to continue this project was my constant visualizing of the end result—the completed *See It. Say It. Do It!* book. My **Ta-Dah!**

I am grateful that you have taken the time to read and use the Activities and strategies to help your child be a successful and confident student. Remember to keep it simple. *See It. Say It. Do It!* is about *Transformation*. If given the opportunity, the best lessons are frequently taught by your child.

I'm reminded of Ryan, who had an amazing collection of the popular toys known as Transformers. With a gleam in his eye, Ryan asked me if I wanted to see him turn into a Transformer. I bit. Before I knew it, he curled up on the floor, and then exploded as he jumped up with his hands raised high yelling, "Look, I'm transformed! **Ta-Dah!**" Indeed he was. And so will your child!

My final thought for you is to have fun. For you. For your child.

See It *Visualize*
+ **Say It** *Declare*
+ **Do It** *Take Action*
———————————————
Ta-Dah! *Transform*

About Vision Therapy and Patient Survey

Vision Overview

The human visual system is complex. The problems that can develop in our visual system require a variety of treatment options. Many visual conditions can be treated effectively with glasses or contact lenses alone; however, some are most effectively treated with vision therapy.

The American Optometric Association (AOA) represents approximately 36,000 doctors of optometry, optometry students, para-optometric assistants and technicians. Optometrists serve patients in nearly 6,500 communities across the country. In 3,500 of those communities, they are the only eye doctors. Doctors of optometry provide two-thirds of all primary eye care in the United States. (*www.AOA.org*)

What is Vision Therapy?

The AOA defines vision therapy as follows:

Vision therapy is a treatment process used to improve vision function. It includes a broad range of developmental and rehabilitative treatment programs individually prescribed to remediate specific sensory, motor and/or visual-perceptual dysfunctions. Vision therapy involves active participation of the patient, under the direction of a doctor of optometry, in a sequence of controlled procedures to modify these functions of the vision system. Therapeutic lenses, prisms, filters, occlusion, and specialized equipment are used in the treatment process. Vision therapy may be used in conjunction with other forms of treatment. Vision conditions commonly treated with vision therapy include amblyopia, strabismus, non-strabismic binocular disorders, ocular motor dysfunctions, accommodative dysfunctions, visual motor disorders, and visual information processing/perceptual disorders.[1]

Vision therapy is administered in the office under the guidance of the optometrist. It requires a number of office visits and depending on the severity of the diagnosed conditions. The length of the program typically ranges from several months to a year. Activities paralleling in-office techniques are typically taught for the patient to practice at home in order to reinforce the developing visual skills.

Children at risk for learning difficulties and possible related vision problems should receive a comprehensive optometric evaluation. This evaluation should be conducted as part of a multidisciplinary approach in which all appropriate areas of function are evaluated and managed.

Vision Therapy Is Not Just Eye Exercise

Unlike other forms of exercise, the goal of vision therapy is not to strengthen eye muscles. Your eye muscles are already incredibly strong. Vision therapy should not be confused with any self-directed program of eye exercises which is or has been marketed to the public. Vision therapy needs to be carefully prescribed and managed by an optometrist.[2]

What Is a Developmental Optometrist?

Developmental optometry (also known as behavioral optometry) is an expanded area of optometric practice that uses a holistic approach in the treatment of vision and vision information processing problems. This type of practice incorporates vision therapy. To find a developmental optometrist who can evaluate and treat your child, refer to the website: *www.COVD.org*.

There are many excellent general optometrists who don't provide vision therapy, but adequately screen and refer for vision problems that require vision therapy. Ask your family optometrist the following questions to determine if he/she is the right person to visually evaluate your child, especially if your child has learning related issues:

- *Do you conduct near-point testing?*

- *Do you give academically related vision testing?*

- *Do you provide vision therapy? If not, do you refer to a doctor who does provide vision therapy?*

What is COVD?

The College of Optometrists in Vision Development (COVD) is an international organization that educates, evaluates and board certifies optometrists in developmental vision and vision therapy. Members of COVD consist of developmental optometrists who have undergone additional specialized education after completing their graduate level professional training in optometry, in addition to vision therapists, optometry students and academicians. Vision therapists also can obtain certification through COVD.

Scientific Research

Research has demonstrated that vision therapy can be an effective treatment option for many vision conditions.[3-9]

The Glossary in *See It. Say It. Do It!* gives further information on these conditions:

- Ocular motility dysfunctions (eye movement disorders)

- Non-strabismic binocular disorders (inefficient eye teaming)

- Strabismus (misalignment of the eyes)

- Amblyopia (poorly developed vision)

- Accommodative disorders (focusing problems)

- Visual information processing disorders, including visual-motor integration and integration with other sensory modalities

There is a strong body of research which supports vision therapy. Numerous scientific studies have been published in journals such as *Optometry and Vision Science, Optometry: Journal of the American Optometric Association, American Journal of Optometry and Physiological Optics, Documenta Ophthalmologica, Archives of Ophthalmology* and *American Journal of Ophthalmology, Journal of Behavioral Optometry, Optometry and Vision Development.*

Review some of those resources, using keywords to search on the following websites at:

- *www.COVD.org*

- *www.visiontherapy.org*

Recently, there have been significant scientific studies which prove the efficacy of vision therapy. One such study is a multi-site large scale randomized clinical study that took 16 years to complete. It was a collaborative effort of optometrists and ophthalmologists funded by the National Eye Institute (NEI). This study revealed that optometric office-based vision therapy is the most effective treatment for children diagnosed with convergence insufficiency (a specific eye teaming/visual efficiency problem).[9]

Is Vision Therapy Just for Kids?

In her book, *Fixing My Gaze,* Susan R. Barry, professor of neurobiology in the Department of Biological Sciences at Mount Holyoke College, clearly writes about how she improved her vision as an adult. Born with crossed eyes, she underwent several eye muscle surgeries, but described herself as stereoblind, never appreciating stereopsis (depth perception). The medical profession believed that her vision never could be improved.

But in her 40s, Barry had vision problems and received vision therapy from an optometrist as an adult. Despite the medical profession's doctrine that a person's vision system could not be improved after a critical cutoff point in a child's development, around age nine, Barry showed great improvement.

Barry describes her story, in clear, lucid and descriptive language—what she personally experienced. Through intensive training and learning, she learned how to align her eyes, fuse their images and regain her depth perception. She describes the beauty of her world changing as her depth perception improved. Simple every day occurrences that most of us would never notice were new and inspirational experiences for Barry—watching snowflakes fall, or appreciating the shapes of flowers in a vase, even the folds in coats hanging on a peg. The uniqueness of this book is that she draws on her personal life experience as well as that of a neuroscientist.[10]

Hellerstein & Brenner Vision Center Patient Survey

A Quality of Life Survey was created in 2009 and sent to vision therapy patients over the previous five years to obtain feedback as to how vision therapy impacted their lives. The survey was anonymous and utilized the on-line tool, *Survey Monkey*.

Questions on the survey included: age of patient, gender, type of referral source, reason for concern/referral, areas of improvements (behavior, symptoms, school, performance, coordination) and overall satisfaction of the vision therapy program.

Survey results indicated that:

- Sixty-one percent of the patients were between ages 6 to 13, with a range of patients from 4 to 75 years old.

- Sixty-eight percent were male, 32 percent female.

- Forty-nine percent of patients were in vision therapy because of learning related issues. The rest were seen for a variety of reasons including eye strain/discomfort, strabismus, coordination problems and brain injury related vision difficulties.

- Over 70 percent of the children in vision therapy for school related problems had difficulty with reading and writing. Work completion, distractibility, math, and spelling concerns were also listed.

- Referrals for vision therapy came from a wide variety of sources including: teachers, tutors, psychologists, physicians (pediatricians, family practice, ophthalmologists, neurologists, ENT, physiatrists), therapists (speech, occupational, physical), optometrists and friends/family.

- Eighty-eight percent reported improvement through vision therapy.

- Improvement was seen in numerous areas, including:

  Academic performance (reading, writing, spelling, math, work completion, increased enjoyment of reading, more independence on homework, less struggling)

  Symptoms (less fatigue, reduced headaches, little or no double vision or blur, more comfort with sustained visual tasks, improved depth perception, eyes straighter)

Behavior (increased ability to concentrate, happier, improved confidence and self-esteem, better attitude, less resistance, more relaxed, improved social relationships)

Coordination (improved fine and gross motor skills, less clumsy, better sports participation, increased balance)

Here are a few of the many responses to the survey question asking for an overall summary of how the vision therapy experience affected his/her life. Some are from the parents, some from the patient.

"My daughter now reads without struggling and without arguing with me to do it. Her confidence has grown tremendously. Also, her ability to concentrate and complete her work is no longer a problem. This has been a great experience for all of us."

"He now reads more quickly and fluently. He went from a child who dreaded reading assignments to one that has a favorite book that he reads just for fun. Work at school and at home does not take as long and therefore he is able to do many other activities. His report card assessment went from being below grade level in some reading and writing areas in 2nd grade to being to straight A's in all subjects in 4th grade! His confidence in his abilities has soared."

"It was an extreme relief to understand that there was a physical cause in my child's school issues and, more importantly, there were concrete steps to improve my child's performance."

"I was able to write more songs and not get frustrated like before. My handwriting got better and I could write more assignments in school. Headaches went away. I am more organized and less frustrated."

"He went from being a non-reader to fulfilling his potential as a high level reader over the course of that one year. His success is school is entirely indebted to it."

"My son is doing better in school and enjoys reading more now."

"I think he had a better attitude about writing because it was easier for him."

"I believe that vision therapy definitely helped my son in many ways. The area he most improved in was reading. The second area was balance and fine motor skills. Sadly, I believe that because we didn't realize the problem until late into his first grade year, his writing fundamentals were not firmly rooted, and we are still struggling with this in fourth grade."

"We spent less time doing his homework and it wasn't such a struggle to get through."

"Reading was always a joy before my accident; post, it became a burden. With therapy, I was able to read again ... and write ... something I wasn't able to do for 18 months."

"The therapy I received greatly improved my functioning. I am now much quicker and more efficient when it comes to my work. Additionally, my eye-strain was greatly reduced which has led to more stamina."

Summing Up

As you can see, vision therapy is utilized for a number of visual conditions. Effective therapy requires visual skills to be developed and integrated with other systems so that the skills become automatic, enabling individuals to achieve their full potential. The goals of a prescribed vision therapy regimen are to achieve desired visual outcomes, alleviate the signs and symptoms of problems, meet the patient's needs, and improve the patient's quality of life. Our survey shows that the latter is not only possible, but is true!

Endnotes

Chapter 1

[1]J. Dispera, *Evolve Your Brain* (Deerfield Beech: Health Communications Inc., 2007).

[2]Jack Canfield, *The Success Principles* (New York: HarperCollins, 2005).

[3]*HealthLetter* 1/08. www.MayoClinic.com.

[4]Jack Canfield, *The Success Principles* (New York: HarperCollins, 2005), 81.

Chapter 2

[1]A. M. Skeffington, "The Low Acuity Emmetrope Who constricted her Visual System," *Clinical Optometry* 45 (1972): 1,3.

[2]Homer Hendrickson, "Vision Development in Man—a Review," *Vision and Learning* (1976), 21-45.

[3]Arnold Gesell, *Themes of His Work* (New York: Human Sciences Press, Inc., 1989), 74.

[4]Howard Gardner, "Wrestling with Jean Piaget, My Paragon," www.edge.org/q2008/q08_1.html#gardner.

Chapter 3

[1]J. Suttie, "Mindful Kids, Peaceful Schools," *Greater Good Magazine* (Summer, 2007), http://greatergood.berkeley.edu/greatergood/archive/2007summer/suttie.pdf.

Chapter 5

[1]George Brandt, *The New Leader 100 Day Action Plan* (Hoboken: Wiley, 2006).

Chapter 6

[1]Jim Vance, *Rock 'N'Roll Seattle Marathon,* 2009.

Chapter 7

[1]D. F. Roberts, U. G. Foehr, V. Rideout, "Generation M: Media In the Lives of 8-18 Year Olds," Kaiser Family Foundation, March, 2005.

[2]B. Tara, "Video Games boost Patient Rehabilitation," *Boston Globe,* June 15, 2009.

[3]American Academy of Child & Adolescent Psychiatry. "Fact for Families #91," 8/06, http://www.aacap.org/cs/root/facts_for_families/children_and_video_games_playing_with_violence.

Chapter 10

[1]Nancy Bell, *Visualizing and Verbalizing for Language Comprehension and Thinking* (Paso Robles: Academy of Reading Publications, 1991), 8-9.

[2]J. K. Rowling, *Harry Potter and the Sorcerer's Stone* (New York: Scholastic Press, 1998), 69.

[3]Reading Plus®/Taylor Associates. www.readingplus.com/main/visagraph.html

[4]Linda Silverman, *Upside Brilliance—The Visual Spatial Learner* (Denver: DeLeon Publishing, 2002), 293.

Chapter 13

[1]Wikipedia. http://en.wikipedia.org/wiki/Mathematics

Chapter 15

[1]C. O'Donnell, "Golden Memories: From the Miracle on Ice to the NHL to the 2002 Olympics-Hockey Digest Tribute: Herb Brooks," *Hockey Digest* (12/03), http://findarticles.com/p/articles/mi_m0FCM/is_2_32/ai_110458295/?tag = content;col1

[2]Alison Arnold, www.screamandrunnaked.com

Chapter 16

[1]Deborah Sandella, *Releasing the Inner Magician—Ways to Find a Peace and Happiness* (Denver: The Inner Magician Series, 2002), www.Innermagician.com

Appendix: About Vision Therapy and Patient Survey

[1]American Optometric Association (AOA). www.AOA.org

[2]College of Optometrists in Vision Development. www.COVD.org

[3]Bowan, Merrill, "Learning disabilities, dyslexia, and vision: A subject review," *Optometry* 73 (2002): 553-75.

[4]Ciuffreda, Kenneth. "The scientific basis for and efficacy of optometric vision therapy in nonstrabismic accommodative and vergence disorders," *Optometry* 73 (2002): 735-62.

[5]Cooper, Jeffrey, "Summary of research on the efficacy of vision therapy for specific visual dysfunctions," adapted from *The Journal of Behavioral Optometry* 9(5) (1998): 115-119.

[6]Maples, W. C., "Visual factors that significantly impact academic performance," *Optometry* 4 (2003): 35-49.

[7]Press, L. J., "The interface between ophthalmology and optometric vision therapy," *Binocular Vision and Strabismus Quarterly* (2002): 6-11.

[8]Suchoff I., Petito G. T., "The efficacy of visual therapy: Accommodative disorders and non-strabismic anomalies of binocular vision," *J Am Optom Assoc* 57(2) (1986): 119-125.

[9]Scheiman, Mitchell, et al., "A randomized clinical trial of treatments for symptomatic convergence insufficiency in children," *Arch Ophthalmol* 126 (2008): 1336-1349.

[10]Barry, S. R., *Fixing My Gaze: A Scientist's Journey Into Seeing in Three Dimensions.* (New York, NY: Basic Books, 2009).

Vision Resource Center

There are numerous resources available for further information on visualization and learning related vision issues. Here are some of my favorites for parents and teachers:

Vision Associations

College of Optometrists in Vision Development (COVD)

215 West Garfield Road, Suite 200

Aurora, OH 44202

330-995-0718 | 888-268-3770

www.COVD.org

Great for information on vision and vision therapy. Excellent referral source for finding a developmental optometrist (Find a doctor).

American Optometric Association (AOA)

243 N. Lindbergh Blvd.

St. Louis, MO 63141

800-365-2219

www.AOA.org

National organization representing optometry in the United States—sets professional standards, lobbies government and other organizations on behalf of the optometric profession, and provides research and education leadership.

Optometric Extension Program (OEP)
1921 E. Carnegie Ave., Suite 3-L
Santa Ana, California 92705-5510
949-250-8070
www.OEPF.org
Resource for books and educational materials on vision.

Optometrists Network
www.Vision3d.com
Resource for research, vision therapy success stories and information on vision.

Neuro-Optometric Rehabilitation Organization (NORA)
www.NORA.cc
Resource for information regarding vision rehabilitation for persons who have physical disabilities and/or traumatic brain injuries (TBI).

Developmental Delay Resources (DDR)
5801 Beacon St.
Pittsburgh, PA 15217
800-497-0944
www.devdelay.org
Resource network integrating conventional and holistic approaches for parents and professionals who support children with special needs.

Suggested Reading

Vision Resources

Berne, S. A. *Creating Your Personal Vision—A Mind-Body Guide for Better Eyesight*. Santa Fe, NM: Color Stone Press,1994.

Barry, S. R. *Fixing My Gaze: A Scientist's Journey Into Seeing in Three Dimensions*. New York, NY: Basic Books, 2009.

Cook, D. *When Your Child Struggles: The Myths of 20/20 Vision*. Atlanta, GA: Invision Press, 2004.

Getman, G. N. *How to Develop Your Child's Intelligence*. Santa Ana, CA: Optometric Extension Program, 1984.

Hoopes, A. M., Applebaum, S. A. *Eye Power: An Updated Report on Vision Therapy*. Charleston, SC: BookSurge Publishing, 2009.

Learning Related

Clark, F& C. *Hassle-Free Homework*. Jackson, TN: Main Street Books, 1989.

Eide, B & F. The Mislabeled Child. *The Mislabeled Child: Looking Beyond Behavior to Find the True Sources and Solutions for Children's Learning Challenges*. New York, NY: Hyperion, 2006.

Furth, H & Wachs, H. *Thinking Goes to School*. New York, NY: Oxford University Press, 1975.

Lane, K. *Developing Your Child for Success*. Lewisville, TX: Learning Potential Publishers, Inc., 1993.

Silverman, L. *Upside Down Brilliance—The Visual-Spatial Identifier*. Denver, CO: DeLeon Publishing, 2002.

Vitale, B. *Unicorns are Real*. Rolling Hills, CA: Jalmar Press, 1982.

Visualization—General

Bandler, R. *Using Your Brain for a Change*. Boulder, CO: Real People Press, 1985.

Belknap, M. *Taming Your Dragons*. Duluth, MN: Whole Person Associates, Inc., 2006.

Forrest, E. *Visual Imagery—An Optometric Approach*. Santa Ana, CA: Optometric Extension Program, 1981.

Gawain, S. *Creative Visualization—Use the Power of Your Imagination to Create What You Want in Your Life*. Novato, CA: Nataraj Publishing, 2002

Lyons, E. *How to Use Your Power of Visualization*. Santa Ana, CA: Optometric Extension Program, 1980.

Kehoe, J, Fischer, N. *Mind Power for Children*. British Columbia, Canada: Transcontinental Printing, 1999.

Willis, J. *How Your Child Learns Best*. Naperville, IL: Sourcebooks, Inc., 2008

Sandella, D. L. *Releasing the Inner Magician—Ways to Find a Peace and Happiness*. Denver, CO: The Inner Magician Series, 2002.

Visualization—Business Related

Canfield, J. *The Success Principles—How to Get from Where You Are to Where You Want to Be*. New York, NY: Harper Publishers Inc., 2005.

Eker, H T. *Speedwealth—How to Make a Million in Your Own Business in 3 Years or Less.* North Vancouver, B.C. Canada: Peaks Potential Publishing, 1996.

Sports Related

Lampert, L. *The Pro's Edge.* Boca Raton, FL: Saturn Press, 1998.

Porter, K. *Visual Athletics*, Dubuque, IA: Wm. C. Publishers, 1990.

Farnsworth, C. *See It & Sink It.* New York, NY: Harper Collins Publishers, 1997.

Glossary of Vision Terms

Accommodation (eye focusing): The ability to focus the eyes to see clearly up close, to change focus from distance to near and back again, and to maintain clear focus for an extended period of time. Poor eye focusing ability can make it difficult to concentrate on reading a book for a long period of time.

Amblyopia (lazy eye): Reduced vision in an eye, not correctable with eye glasses, as a result of the eye not receiving adequate use during early childhood. Most often it results from either misalignment of a child's eyes (strabismus) or a large difference in image quality seen with the two eyes. Over time, the eye with the least clear image is ignored or suppressed.

Binocular vision (eye coordination): The ability of both eyes to work together as a team. Each eye sees a slightly different image and the brain, by a process called fusion, blends the images into one three-dimensional picture. Good eye coordination, a skill that must be developed, keeps the eyes in alignment. Poor eye coordination comes from a lack of adequate vision development or improperly developed control of eye muscles.

Convergence insufficiency: An eye coordination problem in which the eyes have a tendency to drift outward when reading or doing close work. When we read, our eyes have to turn in and they have to point to the same place on the page. If one eye doesn't line up with the other, it can cause problems with reading. Loss of place, loss of concentration, reading slowly, eyestrain, headaches, blurry vision and double vision are common outcomes.

Depth Perception: The ability to judge distances by interpreting size, shape, shadows, and overlapping images.

Developmental (or behavioral) Optometry: A branch of optometry that emphasizes the patient's visual development, function and performance in the context of total behavior. A developmental optometrist takes a mind-body approach to vision and performance—incorporates procedures related to movement, awareness, and stress reduction to achieve better integrated and more effective visual information processing and visual motor function.

Functional integrity of the vision system: The physical health of the eyes, and eyesight.

Ocular motility (eye tracking): The ability to smoothly and accurately move the eyes along a line of print or follow a moving target with our eyes. Poor eye tracking can result in skipping words, losing one's place on a page, having to re-read materials, or difficulty copying from a chalkboard or whiteboard.

Sight: Refers to eyesight or visual acuity.

Strabismus (crossed or wandering eyes): An inability of the two eyes to aim at the same place at the same time. This can result in an eye turning in, out, up or down. A child with crossed eyes may experience periods of double vision and, if untreated, this condition can lead to amblyopia.

Ta-Dah: Transformation part of the VDAT (visualize, declare, action, transform) process. Transformation is about moving or shifting from where you are now to where you would like to be ... it is the process of taking continual steps in your life's journey.

VDAT: Visualize, declare, action, transform. Adult language for *See It. Say It. Do It! Ta-Dah!*

Vision: Refers to seeing, processing and responding to visual information.

Visual efficiency: how well the eyes fixate (look), follow (track), fuse (coordinate together) and focus.

Visual-motor integration (eye-hand-body coordination): The ability to integrate visual information with gross and fine motor movements. Inadequate visual motor integration can result in clumsiness and difficulty with handwriting.

Visual information processing: The process by which the brain interprets and understands the visual information received by the eyes. Aspects include understanding what we see, where things are in space, integration of visual information with other senses, eye-hand-body coordination, visual memory and *visualization.*

Visualization: The ability to imagine, sense, become aware of, move, manipulate and expand the pictures in your "mind's eye" and the feelings or senses in your body, thereby developing new perspectives and creativity.

Sources: www.COVD.org and Dr. Leonard Press

Acknowledgments

This book represents numerous years of experiences and opportunities with many people who have touched my heart. My deepest gratitude and thanks go to:

My writing mentors: Drs. Irwin Suchoff, W.C. Maples and Leonard Press. Without their support, insights and belief in me, I would have never even attempted writing this book. To my tireless and incredible collaborative writer, Dr. Judith Briles—your work ethic, professionalism and integrity took me to a whole new level of writing. Thanks for your boundless energy, trail mix and cherries.

This book was a team effort with the Book Babes as consultants; John Maling, editor; Ronnie Moore for layout; Shannon Parish, Annie Harmon, and Jared Torgerson for illustrations; Cameron Fay and Friesens Printing, and manuscript readers Leonard Press, Nancy Torgerson, Carol Marusich, Irwin Suchoff, Michael Harmon, Mark Simon, Samantha Caldwell and Eric and Michelle Breier. Hugs and thanks to you all.

I have been blessed with many teachers throughout my education and my professional career. I especially want to thank two people who have been very instrumental in my personal transformation. My friend, Cheryl Foster, a spiritual and mindful yoga teacher, who taught me about the breath and the importance of listening to my body; and Dr. Deborah Sandella, my teacher, mentor, coach and friend, for guiding me to walk on the "RIM" and to trust my intuition. To all my healthcare providers who are part of my team in keeping my mind and body healthy; you have shared such beautiful wisdom.

Hellerstein & Brenner Vision Center P.C.: Thanks to my partner, Dr. Tricia Brenner, for her integrity, professionalism, honesty, and a laugh you can hear for miles. To my great staff, you're the best. I couldn't get through a day of work without you. And to my exceptional vision therapists: Traci Collins, Pat Dunningan, Meghan Hayes, Beth Fishman-McCaffrey, Staci Ryman and Cindy Shephard. Together we have built an amazing vision therapy program. Our sharing, teaching and compassion have created one of the top programs in the country. Thanks for your patience, especially through all those planning meetings where I tried my new techniques and strategies with you.

My patients: You are my teachers. Your courage and trust to undertake and complete vision therapy inspired me to create this book and share our successes with others. My gratitude to every one of you.

College of Optometrists in Vision Development (COVD): I received so much from participating on the Board. The friendships, learning, sharing, collaboration, building and success created an incredible experience which I will treasure forever. I appreciate all the great teachers who helped me formulate my philosophy and practice, especially Dr. Robert Sanet who served as my mentor.

My Optometric Study Group: Drs. Beth Ballinger, Dru Grant, Celia Hinrichs, Sandy Landis, Sue Lowe, Carol Marusich, Marcy Rose, Jeri Schneebeck, Nancy Torgerson and Terri Vashe. The many professional and life lessons from all of you are a gift. Your spirit and dedication to our field of developmental vision has made a difference in thousands of lives, including our own.

My beautiful family: Thanks for your love and support. Bruce, "B," your passion and love is contagious. You give new meaning to baseball—a metaphor for life! Annie, your creativity and perseverance has always inspired me to look beyond what's on the paper. Becky, your listening and insights have paved the way for growth and new visions. And to Motts and Potts, thank you for creating a loving family who will always "stick together."

About the Author
Lynn Fishman Hellerstein, O.D., FCOVD, FAAO

As a pioneer in vision therapy, Dr. Hellerstein's expertise and leadership in developmental optometry has inspired thousands of people to improve their vision and enhance their lives. She has extensively utilized vision therapy with children and adults with learning related vision problems, vision perception deficits and/or brain injuries, as well as enhancing visual performance for athletes.

Dr. Hellerstein is known for her electrifying presentations and workshops for parents, educators, therapists, athletes, optometrists, and physicians. She is now utilizing her 30 plus years of vision work to consult with businesses and organizations on how to improve workplace performance through integration of their internal and external vision.

In the nineties, she was appointed to assist in writing guidelines for The Colorado School Vision Screening Interdisciplinary Task Force and Traumatic Brain Injury Task Force of Division of Workers' Compensation. She has published extensively on numerous vision related topics, including a five year optometry/ophthalmology research study utilizing visual electro-diagnostic techniques in patients with traumatic brain injuries. Dr. Hellerstein has also been involved in a school vision development research program in Aurora, CO. She has been a vision consultant for facilities including Health One Spalding Rehabilitation Hospital, Rocky Mountain Multiple Sclerosis Center and Illiff Lifecare Center.

Dr. Hellerstein is the founder of Hellerstein & Brenner Vision Center, P.C., a full-scope optometric practice, located in the Denver Metro area of Colorado. Hellerstein & Brenner Vision Center, P.C. is dedicated to providing the highest quality vision care to patients of all ages. With a highly trained staff and state of the art equipment, her practice strives to go beyond "20/20."

Hellerstein & Brenner Vision Center, P.C. is concerned with prevention, treatment, remediation and enhancement of the visual system for children and adults to achieve optimal function.

Lynn Hellerstein graduated with honors from Pacific University College of Optometry in 1977. She serves as an adjunct professor at Illinois College of Optometry, University of Houston College of Optometry, and Southern College of Optometry.

A Fellow of the College of Optometrists in Vision Development (COVD) and American Academy of Optometry, Dr. Hellerstein is also past president of COVD.

To contact Dr. Hellerstein about presentations or workshops, call or email:
DrH@LynnHellerstein.com
303-850-9499
www.LynnHellerstein.com

To contact Dr. Hellerstein about Vision Therapy:
info@HBVision.net
www.HBVision.net
.7180 E. Orchard Road, Suite 103
Centennial, CO 80111
303-850-9499